# The Complete Australian Cobberdog and Labradoodle

## HANDBOOK AND HISTORY

### Beverley Rutland-Manners

Co-founder and Developer of the
Australian Labradoodle
Australian Cobberdog

2nd Edition Kindle 2016
Biography. 2. Beverley Rutland Manners. 3. Non-fiction.
    4. Labradoodle. 5. Australian Labradoodle.
    6. Australian Cobberdog. 7. Animal husbandry .
    8. Dog breeding. 9. Dog training.

This is a work of nonfiction.

SWEETSPIRE LITERATURE
——— MANAGEMENT ———

# Table of Contents

# Acknowledgement

*This book is dedicated to my family, with a special tribute to my daughter Angela/Mellodie whose vision for a new dog breed with a very special purpose, first set me on my journey to the Australian Cobberdog.*

*My thanks and appreciations go to: my editor for her patience and attention to detail, to the contributors who so generously enriched the content of this book, to the many friends and breeders who have blessed my life over the years with their support and friendship and a very special thank you to the wonderful families all over the world, who have welcomed my puppies into their homes. Without you, none of it would have been possible.*

# Introduction

T his is not the usual book written by a dog fancier about Labradoodles. I have written this book from a unique historical perspective, as
one who took the Labradoodle from its original beginnings, here in Australia, and developed it further into an emerging pure breed.

This book is written for posterity and it is the first time that I have
ever revealed, in such minute detail, the way in which I developed some
of the first cross bred Labradoodles into an emerging pure breed: the
Australian Cobberdog. By documenting this history I also hope to
respond to the myriad of questions that I regularly receive from people
asking me about the Labradoodle, including how and why it is different
to the Australian Labradoodle and where the Australian Cobberdog fits
into the whole picture.

In this book I have also sought to answer other frequently asked questions
in a way that is both entertaining and informative, and which covers issues
such as how to choose the right puppy for your family and the best methods
of raising, training and maintaining this unique breed of dog.

Breeders have not been forgotten throughout the writing of this book
and in its comprehensive breeding section I have striven to answer, in depth,
the most often asked questions which are sent to me by breeders. I have
also added numerous additional tips and guidelines, many of which are

aimed at assisting novice breeders to better understand dog breeding, animal husbandry and to help them set up their own breeding programs.

Some of this handbook's content and breed history is conveyed by true stories of events that I have experienced over the past fifty years during which I have raised, trained, exhibited, developed and bred several pure dog breeds. When referring specifically to the Australian Cobberdog and is ancestors, I describe the sometimes turbulent, triumphant or dramatic events which have transpired during the two decades that I have devoted solely to its development as a new pure dog breed. Where material refers to details of a scientific or medical nature, references are usually provided to academic articles by recognised authorities on the subject.

It is my heartfelt desire that this book may serve to better acquaint families with the delights of the Australian Cobberdog and the responsibilities that accompany sharing their lives with this breed. I also hope that ethical breeders may be inspired to breed the Australian Cobberdog in such a way that the special and unique traits of these exceptional dogs will be preserved for future generations to enjoy.

*Beverley Rutland-Manners*
*Sydney, October 2013*

# Foreword

History has proven that the most successful pioneers in purebred breed development understood from the outset that they needed to set goals and develop methodologies and tools to achieve them.

The continuing development of the Australian Cobberdog has provided new insights and an example of how modern science can be best utilised to achieve a recognisable, predictable breed which has been given every chance at good health and quality of life by incorporating traditional and modern methodologies and science in dog breeding. 'The Complete Labradoodle and Australian Cobberdog' provides information on the history of the breed development and articulates the steps taken to bring it to where it is today.

It is creatively written by someone who understands the purebred dog is a product of vision, thought and sacrifice. It encourages the reader to look beyond science and tradition and search within for inspiration and passion. The author makes owning this breed into a personal and emotional experience for the reader that will take the Australian Cobberdog into a bright future.

This book is a reference for those who have an interest in the breed for its past, present and future. It is filled with inspiration and a reason to awaken our interest in the breed and how it progresses throughout its journey.

Julie Nelson
CEO
Master Dog Breeders and Associates

# Introduction to Dog Politics

B everley Rutland Manners has asked me to write an overview of dog politics, if only to get this somewhat unpleasant topic out of the way before she embarks on the more delightful themes in her book. To ignore the current political climate would not be a complete and honest account of the difficult issues that every high profile and ethical animal breeder faces today. So I hope we can get this topic over with so the reader can move on to the fascinating story of how Beverley has created her enchanting new dog breed.

Sometime in 2008 Beverley came to me for help. If I hadn't been familiar with the issues that she and many others in the animal breeding world were facing, her story of being harassed and receiving death threats would have sounded too far fetched.

Beverley had told me about a group of individuals who were stalking her, breaking into her property at night, photographing and stealing her dogs and setting up hate sites on the internet to destroy her good reputation as a high profile dog breeder. She suspected these individuals and groups were doing this to drive her out of business, but she couldn't, for the life of her, imagine why anyone would do this to her. I advised her that these appear to be illegal activities amounting to: harassment, defamation, theft, destruction of property and trespassing. And I reminded her to report all these activities to the police since they are actionable either under civil and criminal law. I could understand why the motives for the crimes made no sense to Beverley, since she had not done anything to provoke them, but in the brave new world of animal rights and animal liberation extremism where firebombing, murder, violent attacks and break-ins occur on a regular basis against dog and cat breeders, fast food restaurants, circuses, farmers, rodeos, pet shops, horse stables and universities, it was the order of the day. I know that Beverley was having trouble understanding this, as anyone would, and that she was frankly becoming alarmed.

When I first briefed Beverley on some of the current extremist animal rights and animal liberation movements, she seemed confused and told me emphatically that she had always ensured her animals received the best food, accommodation, exercise, love and affection, and vet care available and that her well appointed stud could never have been mistaken for anything other than a quality kennel. She had even donated thousands of dollars to the local chapter of the Humane Society to help prevent animal cruelty and to support animal shelters. Indeed, she mentioned that she had even rescued dozens of animals herself and found loving new homes for them. I told her that this was the way that things were done, once. Since nobody in their right mind would approve of animal cruelty, this is how most people would think about animal welfare - that is: before a radical new animal liberation movement began.

Early in the animal liberation movements (since the 1980s), position statements were made and treatises were written by various activists and organizations outlining a new place and role for animals in society. This included the concept of legally prohibiting animals to be used for any purpose, including as guide dogs or domestic companion animals to humans. PETA

(People for Ethical Treatment of Animals) adopted the following statement from animal rights activist John Bryant as part of their official position: 'The cat, like the dog, must disappear... We should cut the domestic cat free from our dominance by neutering, neutering, and more neutering, until our pathetic version of the cat ceases to exist'. [1] Meanwhile, PETA's founder, Ingrid Newkirk, made this statement: 'I'm not only uninterested in having children. I am opposed to having children. Having a purebred human baby is like having a purebred dog; it is nothing but vanity, human vanity'. [2] As the animal rights movement developed and became influential enough to lobby the government into passing laws that restrict animal ownership, a case was made to elevate animal rights above human rights. Prominent animal rights activist and academic, Tom Regan, specialises in this kind of animal rights theory. When he was asked whether he would rescue a baby or a dog from a capsized lifeboat, Regan answered: 'If it were a retarded baby and a bright dog, I'd save the dog'.[3]

As the animal liberation movement gained more strength, a militant form of compulsory veganism emerged as its central philosophy. This attracted academics as well as the core animal liberation activists who began campaigning for the release of animals from farms into the wild (where animals would often perish), rather than advocating that animals received humane treatment. This philosophy, of course, required that humans no longer eat meat. 'We should distinguish our message from less meat, because what we want is *no* meat,' said Carrie Packwood Freeman, activist and professor at Georgia State University, in 2010.

In their attempt to stop humans eating meat, animal rights extremists have carried out mass break ins and released hundreds of thousands of farm animals into the wild, including turkeys, cows and pigs. Most of these domesticated animals have become either meals for wild predators or encountered painful deaths, such as starvation, since they are not able to fend for themselves in the wild. On December 19, 2006 in Princeton NJ, animal liberation extremists cut fencing at the Griggstown Quail Farm and released 2500 quail, pheasants, and partridges onto a nearby busy highway. Most of the birds were killed in collisions with cars, and while many of their bodies were retrieved, none were found alive. The theft cost the farmer $80 000 and represented a substantial portion of his breeding stock. [4]

By the 1990s the philosophy of animal liberation took on a more dangerous and sinister turn with the 1991 publication: *A declaration of War: Killing People to Save Animals and the Environment.*[5] Since then, escalating violence has occurred against individuals or companies involved with the food and pet industry. Some notable examples are: On September 28, 2006 animal rights extremists in Cambridge, Maryland were suspected of setting fire to the Boston Tropical Fish and Reptile store. On October 31, 2006 arsonists in Standlake, UK torched six fully loaded egg trucks, causing $500 000 in damages. More than 50 fire fighters battled to contain the blaze and tried to prevent it from spreading to nearby buildings where chickens were housed. The Animal Liberation Front (ALF) claimed responsibility for the attack. On April 4, 2006 in Scotchfort, Canada a suspected animal rights activist threw a homemade firebomb into a lobster boat. On August 9, 1999 in Plymouth, Wisconsin the Animal Liberation Front claimed credit for bombing and setting fire to the United Feeds Mill during the morning hours. The damage was estimated as $1.5 million. Another one of hundreds of incidents occurred on January 4, 1997 when over 20 stores and restaurants in Salt Lake City had their windows shot or smashed out, including: McDonalds, Arby's, Kentucky Fried Chicken, a trapping outfitter, a leather shop, milk trucks and other food related businesses. On December 30, 2000, a mail bomb was sent to a pest control company in Cheshire, UK and exploded, injuring the owner's 6 year old daughter who was helping her father with the mail.

These domestic terrorism incidents number in the hundreds and are more comprehensively listed on the website of the National Animal Interest Alliance.[6] Not only do these incidents often go unpunished, but publicizing them brings its own risks, as one UK journalist found out. On October 26, 1999, Graham Hall, an award-winning TV filmmaker was abducted and tortured by animal rights extremists in a sadistic revenge ritual, for exposing the activities of the Animal Liberation Front in his documentary: *Inside The ALF*. Eleven months after the program aired Hall was kidnapped at gun point, blindfolded and driven to an unidentified house where he was bound and told he would be killed. For several hours his assailants tortured him, which included forcing his head between his legs while they burned 'ALF' into his bare back in 4 inch high letters with a hot branding iron. Before releasing him with serious burns and mutilations on his back, extremists threatened to harm Hall's family, torch his house and to kill him if he went to the police. After the incident, the ALF's official spokesperson issued this chilling warning: 'people who make a living in this way have to expect from time to time to take the consequences of their actions'.

After I'd briefed Beverley on the current risks of breeding animals, especially as a high profile person who has created a new breed of dog, she began to understand how fortunate she had really been to avoid more serious harm to herself and to her animals. After being severely harassed by animal rights extremists for several years and after the theft of her most valuable dogs, she was forced to move to an extremely remote location to maintain a safe environment for herself and her dogs. This imposed many hardships on Beverley, but it was the only way she could safeguard the rest of her most valuable bloodlines and ensure her new breed would survive until long after the current social upheavals and madness had ended. This, of course, came at a horrendous price which claimed her business and her home, and threatened to spoil her excellent reputation through the constant defamation she was subjected to on animal extremist's hate websites. Beverley also had to discontinue her time honored traditions of allowing people to visit her kennel.

After paying this horrific and unfair price, Beverley did miraculously succeed in preserving her best bloodlines and is continuing to provide happy, healthy puppies to people in need of stable pets, companion dogs and service animals. Indeed, my wife and I have one of her delightful Australian Cobberdogs as a cherished family pet. Beverley is one of the few individuals to mentally, physically and financially survive such a horrendous attack and she attributes her survival to unwavering faith in a merciful and loving God. She is indeed fortunate to be able to continue, on a small and exclusive scale, breeding the exceptional dog breed that she created.

I was very pleased to let Beverley know that in recent years, much legislation has been passed into law, including the Animal Enterprise Terrorism Act which makes it illegal to interfere with businesses that utilize animals, or to threaten or harass employees or clients of such companies. The Act gives the US Department of Justice and law enforcement wide powers to target Animal Rights extremists and curb their activity. This law is echoed by corresponding laws in several other countries, and I am in close contact with both national and international law enforcement in order to track violations.

Meanwhile, I trust that dog lovers and owners everywhere will go on loving, caring for and enjoying their loyal pets, as they have always done, as their cherished right to bond with humanity's best friend, the dog. Now with the nasty issue of dog politics out of the way, I hope the reader will go on to enjoy the story of how the captivating Cobberdog came into existence.

*Thomas Smith Esq.*
*October 2013*

# Out of the Ashes

The origins of the Labradoodle can be traced back to Australia when in the late 1980's Wally Conron had the inspirational idea of crossing a Poodle with a Labrador. It all started when Wally, as the breeding manager of the Royal Guide Dog Association of Australia, received a letter from a blind woman from Hawaii asking for a guide dog who would not trigger her husband's dog related allergies. In response, Wally tried training a non- shedding, low allergenic Standard Poodle as a guide dog, but when 33 Standard Poodles failed to pass their training over the next three years, Wally's boss pressured him to come up with an idea that actually worked. Finally, Wally threw caution to the wind and mated the Guide Dog Association's best Labrador female to a Standard Poodle male, hoping that the trainability of the Labrador would combine with the Poodle's non allergenic coat and the mix might produce the best of both worlds – a non allergenic and reliable guide dog.

The first cross-bred litter produced just three puppies and when they were five months old Wally had their hair and saliva samples sent to Hawaii to find out if they would affect the client's husband's allergies. Only one puppy from the litter, Sultan, didn't trigger the man's allergies, and before too long the young dog went on to pass his training and was able to start his ten year career as a guide dog for the Association's client in Hawaii.

Meanwhile, Wally continued with his second cross bred litter which resulted in ten puppies, but only three of them had non allergenic coats. After a while, further cross breeding posed a problem for the Royal Guide Dog Association of Australia whose normal practice was to place puppies into private family homes where, for their first year, they lived as pets and were socialised by the family until they were old enough to return for advanced training. But few foster 'parents' were interested in fostering a Lab x Poodle mix, preferring instead to wait for a pure bred Labrador puppy.

In a flash of genius, Wally thought up a catchy name for the unwanted cross breed by combining the Lab and Poodle names to come up with 'Labradoodle' and he told a reporter that this was 'the new Guide Dog Breed'. After the story appeared in the media, hundreds of people called the Guide Dog Association, wanting to foster one of the puppies.

Despite their sudden popularity, Wally's Labradoodle cross breeding program had only mixed success, with a low percentage of dogs that had the desired non-allergenic coats and easy trainability. But instead of continuing with an extensive breeding program that aimed to develop the crossbreeds into an entirely new breed that resulted in dogs with consistent non allergenic coats and trainability, Wally went no further than his early crossbreeding program, and he abandoned it altogether after only a short time. Nor was he particularly happy with his efforts. In a November 13, 2010 article featured in The Guardian, journalist Simon Hattenstone asked 81 year old Wally about his early dog breeding efforts. Conron replied: 'It's not something I'm proud of; I wish I could turn the clock back'.

In spite of Wally's own views of his early work and the abandonment of his novel experiment, the zany looking early Labradoodles had already escaped Pandora's Box and captured the interest of the general public.

Thousands of dog lovers had now seen them at the Guide Dog Open Days and in public places with their puppy walking foster families. Wally's glamorous Guide Dog tag stuck, which continued their appeal with many families who were unaware of the reasons they were no longer being bred as guide dogs.

The experiment that started in Australia would, in a few decades, sweep across the globe but, as Wally further lamented in The Guardian interview, there was a price to pay for their popularity, after hundreds of backyard breeders: 'jumped on the bandwagon, and started crossing any kind of dog with a Poodle'.

It was true that even from the beginning, in the 1980's, the early Labradoodles displayed more than their share of problems. First crosses (F1 being the first cross between a Poodle and Labrador) were unpredictable in appearance and temperament with many being downright odd looking, hard headed and boisterous. Since no experienced dog breeder had yet established a breeding program to consolidate the early crosses into a true breed with consistent conformation and a predictable temperament, the first crossbred Labradoodle owners drew a lottery ticket and never knew, up front, what kind of dog they would end up owning. Despite this, the early Labradoodles had an impelling charm that instantly captivated hearts, including my own.

In early 1990 my daughter Angela had seen some of the 'Doodles', as they were known, at one of the Open Days in Melbourne, and she couldn't wait to tell me about them afterwards. Bursting with enthusiasm, she was utterly convinced that the Guide Dog Association's experimental breeding program had been terminated far too early. She suggested starting where Wally had left off with his crossbreeds, and developing the Labradoodle into a fully- fledged pure breed which reliably and consistently produced the best of its attributes. It wasn't long before I was caught up in Angela's exciting idea. I had been in the dog world for over thirty years by then - breeding, showing and training pedigreed German Shepherd Dogs, Maltese, Scotch Collies, and Shih Tzus, as well as my training and accreditation as a pure breed conformation judge – and thought we had the necessary experience and training to develop a new dog breed.

Especially welcome was a new challenge, since I was already deeply discouraged with the overall health status of the pure breeds I had been involved with over the years. Especially disappointing were the many genetic diseases of purebred dogs, which were impossible to eradicate due to small disease-ridden and inbred gene pools and the turn-a-blind-eye policy of the traditional kennel clubs at that time.

Particularly stricken with genetic diseases were German Shepherds, which carried 89 inheritable diseases and it was rare to see a genetically healthy individual anywhere in the dog breeding world. After devoting 31 years to breeding German Shepherd dogs and trying to genetically improve the breed even without the aid of the genetic health laboratory screening that is available these days, the final straw came when my beloved stud dog 'Rutland' developed anal furunculosis, just one of the dozens of inheritable diseases which are the scourge of this lovely breed. It broke my heart to watch my magnificent stud dog, still in his prime, suffer agonizing pain from repeated surgeries, all to no avail, and I vowed never to breed another German Shepherd dog again.

I will always recall the sad day when I'd hung up my German Shepherd dog leashes. I had sacrificed countless show ring awards by de-sexing some of my best looking animals, all in my pursuit of canine health above all things. And it had all come to nothing, or so I thought. But here was an opportunity to use all my hard earned skills and create a new breed from scratch, thus avoiding the dozens of serious inherited diseases that plague almost all purebreds today.

*Rutland (Grafenburg Just So) and his mother Maedel, both bred by me*

This new project presented more options than I'd ever had before and I was excited by the prospect of creating the new dog breed from 'scratch'. I planned to achieve this by weaving a tapestry of carefully selected bloodlines and using threads of several pure breeds to develop a non- shedding, allergy friendly new dog breed with a non aggressive nature. These dogs had to be gentle enough to be loving and loyal family pets, while being athletic and trainable enough to serve as therapy and service dogs. But above all, I was obsessed with the vision of creating the healthiest dogs on the planet.

Because our ideals embraced so much more than just breeding puppies, my daughter and I recognised that ongoing and extensive research would be necessary over the coming years. This would require meticulous record keeping: for our own reflection, for the new breed and for posterity. With this in mind, Angela set up her Tegan Park Labradoodle Breeding & Research Centre and I founded my Rutland Manor Labradoodle Breeding & Research Centre, named in honour of Rutland (Grafenburg Just So).

During the years that followed, my daughter and I made steady progress in our respective breeding programs. We also made sporadic attempts to combine our efforts and to work together, but philosophical differences eventually saw each of us diverge down our own individual path. Tegan Park bred some beautiful and very special dogs, until Angela ceased breeding in 2009. Angela may well decide to write her own accounting of the way she developed her own bloodlines, but mine had diverged from hers considerably by then.

Over the past 23 years my own breeding program has gone on to develop what is now known as the authentic (Australian) Labradoodle, while I used these bloodlines later to create the Australian Cobberdog, which has been recognized as a pure breed in advanced development. The evolutionary step into the Cobberdog was necessary when the original Australian Labradoodle name was misapplied, by breeders and kennel clubs alike, to crossbreeds of various varieties which did not reflect the original Australian Labradoodle breed development. The Australian Cobberdog has now consolidated into a distinct new breed with its own unique DNA signature. These adorable dogs are consistently intelligent and trainable, with non allergenic fleecy or wool coats, stable temperaments, and ethereal eyes. I will go into greater depth how this breed was created in later chapters of this book.

Meanwhile, back in the early 1990s I could never have imagined that out of the ashes of an abandoned breeding program at the Royal Guide Dog Association of Australia would come the opportunity to create a new dog breed that would just a few years later capture the world's attention and catapult Rutland Manor onto the international stage. But the path to a worthwhile and original vision is never easy, so first a bit about the years of hard work that made the breed.

*Rutlands W.H. Seanna, Australian Cobberdog*
*at four months old – it's in the eyes.*

# Piecing Together a New Breed

C reating an entirely new dog breed is a daunting challenge that relatively few persons have ever achieved successfully, considering there
are only 157 breeds recognised by the American Kennel Club and around
5000 pure breeds in development, since domestic dog breeding began. On
second thought, after my initial enthusiasm, I was unsure if I would succeed in such an ambitious task and first I had to reflect on each aspect of
the challenge.

In my view, developing a new dog breed must address a specific need that
an existing breed is unable to meet. It should also serve a higher purpose, as I
hope my own vision has, of providing a reliable companion dog with a non
allergenic coat to families, children and people with disabilities.

Once the potential new breed's purpose is established, it can't be
created by simply crossing two breeds together or even continuing to
breed the resulting mixed breed offspring together. This would eventually
lead to a genetic dead end which has already resulted in the genetic health
deterioration evident in so many dogs. While the media has dubbed the
offspring of crossing two breed as 'designer dogs' it has given no attention to
the skills and resources required to develop an entirely new dog breed with

a unique and uniform genetic signature and healthy DNA. It takes decades of selective breeding before a unique breed standard is established and the offspring start to breed true to type and display the uniform appearance and stable temperament typical of its pure breed.

Breeding true to type is extremely important since it ensures the new owners can know what to expect from their pure bred puppy, especially if they require a reliable special purpose dog such as a guide dog. On the other hand, potential dog owners who do not require a special purpose dog breed or a non-allergenic breed are in an ideal position to adopt a dog from a shelter.

Once I was committed to developing a special purpose, non allergenic companion dog breed, I needed to chart the course with a breeding plan. I was looking for one or more suitable pure breeds to add (infuse) to the early Lab x Poodle crosses. It had to be a pure breed that could contribute certain desirable qualities and breed true to its own breed standard. If I'd added a cross breed to a developing new breed which wasn't stable in its own type, the variables would be like throwing random pieces of a puzzle into the air and expecting all the desirable attributes to emerge purely by chance, which of course is next to impossible. So, with Mendel's Laws of Inheritance in mind, I hoped that infusing a suitable pure breed into my early multi generation Lab x Poodle crosses would provide at least some assurance of what I could expect in the generation following the infusion, but more about that later in this chapter.

After my previous experience with breeding pure bred dogs, I wanted to begin my new breed with as clean a genetic slate as possible by selecting the healthiest individuals I could find to serve as a foundation for the new breed. Before DNA testing became widely available, I had to rely on selective breeding, strict monitoring and record keeping, right down to details such as: were they good eaters? Did they breed easily? (Some pure breeds have been so weakened that they cannot mate or give birth naturally). Were the females good mothers? These qualities were essential for the future breed's survival.

In the breed development phase, most of the puppies were spayed and neutered to become pets for families in need of stable and non allergenic companion animals, while I continued evolving the breed with only a few of the most outstanding individuals to guarantee the emerging breed's robust mental and physical health over time. My early efforts were later fully vindicated when it was discovered that the Labradoodle had the most genetically healthy DNA of all the major dog breeds tested.

Apart from the difficult decisions about which pure breeds to infuse, I came to realise that breeders developing new breeds have a long and difficult journey to gaining purebred status, since no infusion is allowed for at least four generations, before puppies can be regarded as purebred, after which the progeny are expected to breed true to type and conform to the new breed's standard. In the world of breeding and juggling infinite genetic variables, this is a big ask, but possibly the biggest obstacle to new breed recognition comes from the red tape of the dog breeding associations themselves.

During the earlier stages in the creation of the Australian Labradoodle, it was still considered a cross-breed. In the 1990s there was no place to register non pure breeds and no reliable and trustworthy database existed to keep track of breeding records. This was difficult for someone like me, who was developing a new breed, since in those days most kennel clubs weren't set up for that eventuality. The American Kennel Club (AKC) initiated a registration system many years later for new breeds in development, but that wasn't always the case in Australia. As of 2013, the Australian National Kennel Council (ANKC) still makes no realistic provision for new breeds, but fortunately the progressive Master Dog Breeders and Associates (MDBA) does make provision for emerging breeds, as it is an international pure breed dog registry with its headquarters in Australia.

However, despite the early obstacles I always intuitively knew that every step in the development of the Australian Labradoodle was of great significance, and I recorded every dog I bred with my own prefix of 'Rutlands' preceding the rest of its name. When I purchased a breeding dog from someone else to infuse into my breed or to widen the gene pool, I named that dog 'so and so OF Rutland Manor', or 'so and so OF Rutlands' to show that I had not bred the dog, but that it had been used to further develop the breed at the Rutland Manor Labradoodle Breeding and Research Centre in Australia.

In the 1990s the early Lab Poodle crosses and second generation 'Labradoodle' crosses were mostly large dogs, with black noses, long snouts, dark eyes and nondescript coats that were either hair coats that shed, or wool coats that didn't. Some hair coats were short like a Labrador, or scruffy looking like Irish Wolfhounds. Temperaments ranged from hard headed and willful to excitable and hyperactive. Yet beneath the obvious, and somewhat random, genetic traits, which were still in flux and had not set into a type, lurked the more complex challenge of avoiding the unexpressed genetic diseases that were carried by both of the foundation breeds, the Labrador and Poodle.

*Typical early first cross between Labrador and Poodle*

As mentioned, when I started my Labradoodle breeding program in the early 1990s undiagnosed genetic diseases were rife in every dog breed and genetic screening was not yet available to guide me in my breeding decisions. Since I was determined to identify and weed out as many genetic faults as possible in my animals, I took them to the vet for X-rays to screen for hip and elbow dysplasia, but apart from that, I really had to just 'try it and see' to learn which bloodlines were carrying disease or other major faults and which weren't. If a puppy later developed an inherited disease, I bred the mother to a different male, and vice versa, in an attempt to discover which parent was carrying the defect and once I knew this, I stopped breeding from the dog with the affected bloodline. These arduous test- matings were slow to reveal the origin of problems and it was extremely disappointing and often emotionally difficult for me to terminate the bloodline of a genetically flawed animal I had grown to love. But I did this responsibly by removing the animal from the breeding program, having it de-sexed and placing it in a pet home where the new owner was aware of the problem if it was likely to surface in that individual, and was prepared to take on the associated responsibilities.

Out of these early trials began emerging standards for the new breed. To accomplish the uniformity required for establishing stable breed standards, I devised strict criteria for selecting breeding animals. In order of importance they had to display:

1.  Soundness in mind and body (physical and emotional stability and health).
2.  Conformation relating to form-to-function; the ability to easily carry out the physical purposes for which the breed was designed and created, without pre-disposition to stress related injury from inappropriately formed bodily structure.
3.  Consistency of breed 'type'.

4.  Coat Type – fleece or wool (selected for allergy friendliness, non-shedding and easy maintenance).

To create the Australian Labradoodle, as it is known today, I used several pure breed infusions to set its type and conformation. This information has not been previously published, but I've included it here to set any misconceptions straight and to create an accurate historical record of how the Australian Labradoodle started.

Once the multigenerational Labradoodles were genetically stable (and only then) did I select my infusions. It is most important to ensure the stability of the foundation stock first or else all ground will probably be lost after the infusion and the offspring will end up with huge variations in type. The idea is not to crossbreed, but to infuse, and there is a huge difference. The infusion should bring desirable qualities without disturbing the stability of the type.

I chose the Irish Water Spaniel for the first infusion since this robust breed ticked all the boxes for me, especially when I found out a few years later that it had fewer inherited diseases than either the Labrador or Poodle parent breeds of the early Labradoodle. [7]

I also chose the Irish Water Spaniel because the breed was used extensively for retrieving in the field, and I was particular in selecting an infusion from working field trial dogs, rather than show ring champions. This choice dates back to my career as a show judge when I appraised hundreds of dogs being shown in conformation classes, where the owner trots it around in a small show pen for a couple of minutes to demonstrate its movement, and then 'stacks it' (stands it up in a posed stance) to present the best positive traits of the dog to the judge in the most advantageous way. I noticed then that a clever handler can disguise faults in the dog by strategic stacking and can even interfere with its workout to hide movement issues. Show champions are bred because of their show ring achievements alone, but in order for field trial working dogs to be worth breeding from they must have proven themselves first in the field. A field working dog is assessed on its endurance and ability to work all day which involves running up and down gullies and hills, through thick underbrush, and swimming in deep water to retrieve birds. Its temperament is tested by noisy gunfire and its physical stamina and willingness to work away from its handler tests its intuition and suitability for its origin of purpose.

This first infusion of the Irish water spaniel, added an extra 30% pure breed into the original recipe, and contributed its soft retrieving mouth, a non shedding coat and gentle nature, to the emerging Australian Labradoodle. It was also responsible for introducing two new colours: Chocolate and Raven (black). Standard Poodles had, by now, brought in the brown gene, but the puppies usually paled out to Café au lait at maturity, while those with Irish Water Spaniel heritage tended to retain their rich chocolate coat colour well into maturity. Colour-fastness is especially important since, in sunny and hot climates, weathering or sunburn bleaches the outer edges of brown coats to a bronze colour, and Chocolates are sometimes mistaken for Café au lait. But when the coat of an Irish Water Spaniel derived Australian Labradoodle is parted, the deep chocolate colour is clearly visible for two or three inches from the skin.

*Irish Water Spaniel*                *Cobberdog-Chocolate underneath*

While the Irish Water Spaniel infusion moved the emerging Labradoodle breed farther away from the Labrador's hair coat influence, making the non-shedding coats more reliably consistent, it also introduced the Spaniel's hairless 'rat tail' and a few other characteristics that took me some time to eradicate. Fortunately, the 'rat tail' disappeared over the next generation or two, but the bald face and short haired muzzle reappeared from time to time in much later generations. I concluded that they must be carried on a recessive gene since they would pop up unexpectedly after having skipped several generations. Despite this, the new breed was starting to take shape and the de-sexed puppies that I had decided not to eventually breed from were starting to become very popular with families wanting a gentle and predictable pet.

*'Ziggy' a fine example of a smooth face pattern*
*and flat coat- with special friend*

In order to dilute the genes for smooth faces, I decided to introduce fresh genetic material and infuse another pure breed into progeny from the Irish Water Spaniel. Around that time there was an increasing demand for a much smaller Australian Labradoodle and I back bred some large females to a Miniature and Toy Poodle. Predictably, the size did come down, and the instances of bald faces dramatically decreased, but I wasn't completely happy with all of the puppies from these matings; their bone structure was much finer and underneath their pretty coats, they had pointed and narrow faces which restricted the sinuses and didn't fit my vision for a healthy breed. Also, just as I was succeeding in eliminating the genetic problems of the core breeds, I found that the Toy Poodle back breedings introduced slipping patellas (kneecaps) into the offspring, so I discontinued the affected line and started looking for a different small pure breed to infuse.

*Back-breeding to Miniature Poodle*     *American Cocker Spaniel Infusion*

For this downsizing stage, my breed of choice to infuse was the English Cocker Spaniel. I knew that in using a hair coated dog I risked losing some ground I'd gained with coat quality and I expected some of the resulting puppies to be hair coated and shedding. But I decided to risk it anyway in hopes of regaining the lost bone structure in the Mini and Toy Poodle progeny, since I could always select the best coated puppies to breed on with.

By then I had the benefit of Dr Jean Dodd's research which showed the number of inheritable diseases that each pure dog breed carried in its DNA. I learnt that 59 inheritable diseases were occurring with more than expected frequency in the Labrador, 40 in the Standard Poodle, and 59 in the Miniature Poodle. This vindicated my choice, since the English Cocker Spaniel had one of the lower rates of most other breeds at 25. [8]

When the puppies arrived, I was pleasantly surprised when non shedding coat quality was not lost with this infusion, which I put down to the heavy Poodle influence from the back breeding. But overall the body and bone substance had not been corrected in the way I had hoped.

To counteract the narrow heads and finer bone, for my next infusion I used an American Cocker Spaniel sire, whose first generation puppies were exactly what I'd hoped for with solid substance, sturdy bone structure and above all, the nice broad heads were back. To set the type even more, I used only one American Cocker Spaniel for a single mating to prevent any amplification of the higher levels of inheritable diseases this breed variation has as opposed to the lesser numbers in the English Cocker Spaniel.

A few generations after these infusions, my Australian Labradoodles were really starting to look exceptional and were breeding uniform and true to type as an emerging pure breed. The puppies were in high demand in Australia, Europe and the USA. Many breeders ordered stud dogs from me to start their own Labradoodle breeding program in other countries. I also noticed that so many of the puppies were starting to display heightened intuition, trademark clear eyes, a wise look and a distinct preference for human company as opposed to their litter mates.

*Rutland's hallmark Australian Labradoodle wise puppy look*
*THE DOODLE CRAZE BEGINS*

Before too long I was inundated with invitations to go overseas after exporting my puppies to more than a dozen countries around the world. In 2000 I began bi-annual 'Doodle' tours throughout the USA. Sometimes I covered 10 cities over 6 weeks in a hectic and exhausting schedule, made easier by my gracious American hosts who took me into their hearts just as they had embraced my dogs. Hundreds of dog lovers enthusiastically attended my free clinics, seminars and workshops. Many families traveled across America, flying or driving with their dogs, to be at these events, and I was fortunate to be able to meet so many of them, hear their stories, handle their dogs and record valuable data about how the breed was developing .

*80 Australian Labradoodles attended this Romp, hosted
by Sandy and Sue-Ann Singer (pictured sitting beside
me) Hidden Hills California September 2006*

In 2006 I was fortunate to be in California just as a consignment of my home bred puppies arrived at LAX from Australia. In fact, they were on my flight and I was able to see them shortly after they were unloaded. When I saw, with my own eyes, the wonderful condition they were in after a 15 hour flight from Australia I didn't ever worry again about sending my puppies overseas. As they exited their travel kennels with wagging tails and ready to make friends, it was all the proof I needed that my method of preparing them for travel was working. They were soon happily united with their new owners and everybody was ecstatic, including the puppies.

*Meeting the Comfort Stop crew and the puppies' new
families on arrival at LAX from Australia*

Feedback from Australian Labradoodle owners was exceptionally positive concerning the puppies' allergy friendly and non-shedding coats, stable temperament, intuition and trainability. But my breeder's eye wasn't happy yet with the breed's overall conformation. I noticed that the top lines (backs) especially of the larger dogs, were becoming long and slack, and 'slung' between withers and croup, with subsequent weakness over the loins which could pre-dispose to hip dysplasia and other OCD's (joint abnormalities) down the track, if allowed to continue in breeding pools. My dogs had also inherited the hairy ear canal of the Poodle and the heavy ear flap of the Labrador, traits which predisposed all Labradoodles to ear infections. In addition, the coats on the majority of the dogs were thick, dense and high maintenance.

On returning back home to Australia after one of my tours, I pored over my notes and studied the photos and videos I had taken. I wanted to find out which bloodlines were predominantly producing the weaker traits I'd found and I was disappointed to find that they were widespread throughout the Australian Labradoodle population. I hadn't planned on adding another infusion to the breed but unless I did, there was no way of improving the Australian Labradoodle to an even higher level of health and functionality. According to my notes, owners were delighted with their dogs' overall nature and behaviour in diverse situations and environments, and I certainly didn't want to risk losing those hard won and exceptional characteristics that made the dogs ideal as companion and service dogs. Any more infusions would be a delicate balancing act between structural soundness and inherently positive and stable character traits.

At this stage of the Australian Labradoodle's emergence, its personality and its non-shedding and allergy friendly coat were as firmly set as possible, considering the breed was still in development, so I didn't think that these traits were in danger of being compromised. The breed I would decide on for the final infusion needed above all else, to have consistently reliable conformation. The skeletal structure of a dog is the framework upon which muscle, ligaments, tendons and even fat distribution are built and supported. The final infusion into the Australian Labradoodle would be expected to correct conformational weaknesses and eliminate, or at least reduce, any tendency toward chronic ear infections.

It would be an ambitious project, but in August 2004 I summoned my courage and infused the Soft Coated Wheaten Terrier into two of my established bloodlines. [9] I had selected the Irish Soft Coated Wheaten especially for its compact structure, lovely straight limbs, strong back, its overall balance and light silky coat. I also hoped that its elevated ear carriage close to the head would raise the pendulous ears of the Australian Labradoodle, thus improving air flow, which I hoped would reduce or even eventually eliminate the tendency toward ear infections. The two animals I chose came exclusively from pure Irish bloodlines, since the Irish founders of the breed had stringently protected it from the diseases and exaggerations which have changed the non Irish lines across the world. The Irish bloodlines also carried 75% fewer hereditary diseases than most other breeds. [10] (I was also aware of some temperament issues that had infiltrated some of the non-Irish bred dogs, and in my opinion only breeders of the pure Irish lines had held true to the integrity of the breed's origins.) My only remaining concern was that the feisty temperament of the Terrier would dominate over the already established gentle and intuitive nature of my Australian Labradoodle bloodline.

I bred two infused litters: one Irish Soft Coated Wheaten Terrier stud dog was bred by A.I. (artificial insemination conducted by a specialist veterinarian) to a Standard wool coated female Australian Labradoodle, Rutlands Funnie Bunnie, and an unrelated Irish Soft Coated Wheaten was also bred by A.I. to an unrelated Miniature wool coated female, Rutlands Lil Misty. Just over two months later, Bunnie had eleven puppies and Misty had eight.

Just one glance at the litters told me that I needn't have worried about a thing. The improvements were spectacularly successful, already in the first generation of the infusion. The offspring were robust, well balanced, with higher set ears and beautiful silken coats which gave rise to the fine fleece coats that they are known for today. Not only did all the conformational improvements come through, but the Terrier nature did not, leaving the Australian Labradoodle with its eager-to-please gentle nature. And to top it all off, the breed maintained its non allergic qualities and no longer suffered from a tendency toward ear infections. A robustly healthy dog meant fewer vet expenses for owners, while the light and silky fleece coats required less maintenance and grooming.

*Irish Soft Coated Wheaten Terrier*

This final infusion had carried the developing Australian Labradoodle breed forward towards my original vision of a robust, gentle, stable, non allergenic and genetically healthy pet, therapy dog or assistance dog. An extra bonus was the speed with which the emerging breed was setting and stabilising to the breed standard. For the first time, I was seeing stunninguniformity in the puppies, and prospective owners would be thrilled to find that with Australian Labradoodles, what you see is exactly what you get.

*Breed uniformity in Rutlands Australian Labradoodles*

## THE NEW WORKING DOGS

Since I had succeeded in developing a stable dog breed thus far, I wanted to test them out for service work, so I donated two puppies to Susan Leuhrs, founder and principal of Hawaii Fi-Do, a service dog training facility in Hawaii. Susan named them Max and Mattie, and she was eager to trial the Australian Labradoodles for service work and when Mattie and Max passed her rigorous training program in record time both were placed with clients as working service dogs. Susan and I were both thrilled with the results and I donated adult breeding stock to Hawaii Fi-Do to enable them to commence their own breeding program, which turned out many more successful service dogs.

Susan Leuhrs' assessment of the breed as Service Dogs was particularly rewarding to me and showed me that my vision for the new breed was becoming a reality. This is what she put on record:

# ASSESSMENT OF AUSTRALIAN LABRADOODLES AS SERVICE DOGS

*The Australian Labradoodles have been wonderful dogs for the field of service dogs. Their temperament, trainability, intelligence and bonding are some of the key qualities the industry requires to certify a dog. This breed has it all and more with their non-shed and allergy free coats.*

*Hawaii Fi-Do has been using the majority of the Australian Labradoodles for children due to their gentle nature and whimsical personalities. Our dogs have been placed working as physical assistance/mobility dogs, asthma alert, therapy/companion and autism dogs in addition to working in the community going into hospitals, care home and elementary school.*

*Susan Leuhrs.*

*Mattie and Max, Hawaii Fi-Do's first donated
service dog puppies in Hawaii 2004*

*Lineup of eight Certified Assistance Dogs from
Hawaii Fi-Do's Breeding Program*

A few years after my Australian Labradoodles' successful debut as service dogs, DNA health testing became commercially available to dog breeders. In 2007 I immediately jumped on board and had all my dogs tested. After I had spent the past 15 years applying such rigorous health standards to my breeding program I could hardly wait to find out, with scientific precision, exactly where my new breed stood with regards to genetic health. The genetic tests came back clean, one after the other, and the very occasional dog with a hidden predisposition toward a genetic disease would be culled out of my bloodlines, neutered and placed with a family (who was aware of the issue and willing to accept the responsibility) as a pet. It must be said that a defect can occasionally come through, even with the most rigorous testing available, since not every defect can be detected in the genetic screening. However, from then on, I subjected all my breeding animals to extensive genetic testing (between 28 and 54 genetic diseases) and I am listed as an approved breeder with the Veterinary Genetic Assurance program (VGA), an organisation that works with veterinarians and breeders to further the practice of genetic health screening in dogs. [11]

Over the ensuing years, I had always wondered how this emphasis on genetic health had impacted Labradoodles since so much of my breeding stock has influenced Labradoodle breeding as a whole. My answer came in the May 2011 report of world-renowned veterinary research scientist Dr Jean Dodds who has expertise in canine hematology, immunology, endocrinology and nutrition. Her report is designed to catalogue the identified congenital and hereditary disorders found in pure bred dogs that are known to be genetic in origin, because they appear with higher than expected frequency, or because the flawed genetics have been documented in the referenced scientific literature. I was interested to find that, just as I'd suspected, one of the breeds with the highest numbers of genetic defects was the German Shepherd, and among the lowest listed (with the exception of the American Cocker Spaniel) were the breeds that I had infused while developing the Australian Labradoodle.[12]

The greatest news of all was that the Labradoodle had the lowest incidence of defects among all dog breeds, which I thought could only be the end result of careful and responsible selection during breeding. After 20 years I felt that my vision of creating the healthiest dog of all was finally being realised.

# Hollywood Stars and Stormy Skies

O ver the fifty plus years that I have spent as a dog breeder, including several years as a licensed conformation judge, I have seen the popularity of a number of dog breeds come and go, but never before have I witnessed anything close to the Australian Labradoodle's meteoric rise to fame and sustained global popularity. Before its current level of recognition, 'doodle' was an affectionate term used exclusively to describe the Australian Labradoodle. But after its reputation swept around the globe like a tidal wave, people reported that strangers pulled them up in public to ask what breed of dog they had, where they'd got it from and could they have their photo taken with it. A huge demand for 'Doodles' seemed to open overnight and the scam artists started getting in on the act to supply the market with anything and everything they could crossbreed. Since the original Australian Labradoodle was still so rare, and most people had never seen one, thousands of nondescript cross bred fluffy puppies emerged from puppy mills and backyard breeders and were passed off as the original Australian Labradoodles, in pet shops and newspaper advertisements. Before too long, any Poodle mix was tagged a 'doodle'.

These scams were first brought to my attention when I received a frantic telephone call from Yvonne[*] , a young mother whose husband had brought home what a pet shop sales assistant had told him were two Australian Labradoodle puppies, as presents for her and their two young boys. Their younger son, Ricky[*] , was an asthmatic, and so allergic to dog hair that he broke out in a rash and had difficulty breathing as soon as he cuddled the supposedly allergy friendly puppies that his father had bought. Yvonne was highly agitated and flat out angry when she phoned me while she was waiting for the ambulance to arrive. 'You have to stop telling people that these dogs are allergy friendly!' she yelled. 'I've had to call an ambulance and you might have killed my son!'

I could understand her distress after what had happened, but frankly I was perplexed, so I did my best to calm her down to get a brief account of her story. She told me that Ricky had longed for a puppy since he was old enough to speak, but was so allergic to dogs that it had been out of the question. His father had paid the pet shop a thousand dollars each for the two sibling puppies, she said, after the sales assistant had told him that they were 'hypo-allergenic' Labradoodles. After hearing her out, I wished her good luck at the hospital and asked her to call me after they'd returned from the ER to let me know how her son was. When Ricky was safely home with preventative medication, in case it happened again, she did call me back, and asked if she could bring the two puppies to me for my appraisal. She had been looking at pictures of my dogs online, and now she wasn't sure if the pet shop puppies really were Australian Labradoodles.

The next morning Yvonne arrived with two pretty long haired puppies. They were cute carbon copies of each other and probably came from the same litter, but they were most definitely not Labradoodles of any kind. At that time, there were no patched colours in the developing breed, and these two had splashes of white through their tan and black coats. Quite apart from their appearance, their coats were hair textured and completely unlike the fleece or wool of Australian Labradoodles. I suggested that she return them to the pet shop and ask for a full refund and advised her not to take no for an answer, since the pet shop had misrepresented their breed and placed her son at risk. I also reassured her that if necessary, I would be her witness if she wanted to take the matter further.

The following afternoon, Yvonne called again to tell me that the woman in the pet shop had been defensive, and when she was told what I had said, she'd replied sourly; 'and what would *she* know', meaning me of course. But Yvonne stuck to her guns and got her refund. She wanted to see what Ricky's reaction would be to my dogs before putting herself on my waiting list for a puppy, so a few weeks later she came with her husband and both children, armed with a nebuliser and oxygen machine. I began the visit, as I always did in those early days, by sitting them down in a room isolated from the main house that was kept free of cat or dog dander, while I held an adult dog (Anna Lise) on a leash at the opposite end of the room, several meters away from the family.

As I chatted with the family, Anna Lise lay quietly at my feet, and when I observed that Ricky was showing no discomfort, I inched the dog just a bit closer to where the boy sat. I repeated this procedure a few more times until we were right beside the little boy's chair. Again, Ricky showed no adverse reaction. Next, I kneaded my fingers deep into Anna Lise's luxurious coat for a few moments, before laying my same hand on Ricky's bare arm, asking him to let it rest there, provided he wasn't itchy or feeling any of his allergy symptoms, in which case he was to tell me immediately. His mother looked nervous, but she didn't interfere, and I was touched by the trust she was placing in me. Ricky looked both anxious and excited, but he did everything he was asked, while his gaze was fixed on Anna Lise. I could see that he was aching to touch her.

'What would normally happen if Ricky was so close to a dog for this period of time?' I asked his parents. When they replied that he would already have broken out in a rash, I knew it was time to take the next step. I looked directly into the child's eyes and said earnestly: 'Ricky, would you feel comfortable if Anna Lise walks up to you and places her head on your knees?' He nodded vigorously. 'Call her to you, then', I suggested and watched as the dog took the cue to go to the boy. I observed Ricky closely as he stroked her big cream Labradoodle face and silky ears, while she half closed her lustrous dark eyes from his touch. The memory of the child's blissful face as he fondled and patted a dog for the first time in his life, without any adverse reaction, will stay with me for my lifetime.

Things were going so well, that it was time to bring in Captain to meet Ricky. The big male Chocolate Labradoodle was a licker and kisser, unlike Anna Lise who was less demonstrative and better suited to therapy work where licking is not allowed. True to character, Captain waltzed over to each family member, with tail wagging and his dishcloth tongue going licketty spit. Everyone fell in love with the big brown dog and soon Ricky and his brother were in fits of giggles while Captain showed off and played to the audience. This exercise made it clear that Ricky displayed no allergy to dog saliva (nor to the non-hair fleece of my Australian Labradoodles) and he ended up joining his brother on the floor, tumbling around with Anna Lise and Captain, with the boys burying their faces in the dogs' coats and having the time of their lives. The visit was an outstanding success and a few months later Yvonne and her family came to visit again; this time to pick up their very own Australian Labradoodle puppy.

While still developing the Australian Labradoodle breed, I made it standard practice to test any potential buyers whose allergies were triggered by dogs, before allocating them a puppy. I did this either by sending them a sample of my dogs' fleece or by testing them in close contact as I had done with Ricky. Over several years of conducting these tests, hundreds of individuals who usually had allergies triggered by dog hair found their allergies were not triggered by the fleeces of my specially bred Australian Labradoodles. However, there were around six individuals who displayed allergies even to those fleeces and it needs to be said that some people will react to all dogs regardless of the breed and they need to avoid contact with all dogs. Overall however, it seemed that my careful breeding selection process had in fact succeeded in developing an allergy friendly dog! Over the next few years, however, I was alarmed when I discovered that many breeders and puppy mills were breeding Labs to Poodles, and claiming their dogs were hypoallergenic. There is no such thing as a hypoallergenic dog, and allergy friendliness is not commonplace in the first cross Lab cross Poodle. Such false claims put the public at unnecessary risk and so it is essential for potential dog owners to source their Labradoodle puppy from a knowledgable breeder who uses proven bloodlines and who recognizes the coat types on the dogs they breed.

By the late 1990s word of the emerging breed of Australian Labradoodles traveled even more widely, and my dogs and I were featured on several television shows, including the ABC's Creature Features, National Geographic, Channel 7's Talk to the Animals, and a number of other broadcasts.

*Filming with National Geographic*

The publicity, however, was double edged. On one hand it was beneficial for hundreds of families to know about and own such a trainable, stable and gentle pet or therapy dog, and for those with allergies to dog hair to discover that the Australian Labradoodles did not trigger their allergies. But the more publicity the authentic Australian Labradoodle got, the more its reputation was compromised by thousands of breeders who were randomly crossing various breeds with Poodles in an attempt to cash in on the Labradoodle's popularity and good reputation by using its name. This hit and miss breeding resulted in many hair coated shedding dogs with unstable and unpredictable temperaments and odd conformation, many of which ended up in animal shelters because their owners either couldn't control their hyperactive natures, or else the dog's shedding hair triggered their allergies. Some dogs, who were lucky enough to escape going to an animal shelter and being euthanized, were the ones brought to me for retraining and re-homing. But I found it particularly stressful to watch families say goodbye to the dogs they loved but couldn't keep, and depart down the driveway with everyone in tears while I held an upset dog that was straining desperately on the leash and wanting to follow them. I think it's fair to say that by opposing puppy mills and backyard breeding practices since the early 1990s I was one of the first animal welfare campaigners and dog rescuers, before those activities were fashionable, as they are today. In fact, I established the first Labradoodle rescue in the world.

In those days I hated to turn anyone away, but eventually it was too much for me to handle due to the large numbers of dogs being brought to me and I had to learn to say no. I vowed though, that I would fight for as long as I had breath in me, to save the beautiful companion dog breed that I had developed and continue a blood line of authentic Australian Labradoodles with a unique genetic signature. This involved educating as many people as possible about the genuine Labradoodle and the pitfalls lying in wait for those who may buy counterfeits.

By the late 1990's the Labradoodle was so popular-and fraudulent practice so commonplace that my daughter and I wanted to come up with another way of safeguarding our fledgling breed. In 2000 we founded the world's first registry for the Labradoodle in an effort to provide it with some protection. We named it the Labradoodle Association of Australia (LAA) and its historic official gatherings were held in Melbourne [13] and we recorded these events with photographs and videos which are now in our archives.

*The first Labradoodle association in the world*

As the Labradoodle craze spread throughout Australia, the public couldn't get enough of 'Doodles', and owners were so eager to show off theirs, that scores of groups organised get-togethers on weekends to socialise with their dogs and each other. These events became known as 'Doodle Romps', and they ranged from informal private gatherings aimed at making new friends while the dogs romped and played, to well organised and catered public events. I accepted invitations to as many romps as I was able to manage in Australia, and I loved demonstrating grooming and training to the folk who were experiencing their first pet dog due to their allergies.

*Grooming demonstration April 21, 2001 at Perth, Western Australia*

Over the decades, I also hosted many other Doodle Romps at Rutland Manor, my own 202 acre Victorian property where dogs could frolic around on manicured lawns and idyllic parklands.

I had spent all my energy and sank my entire life savings into building Rutland Manor, the first facility of its kind in the world that included hotel like lodging for dogs with individual heated kennels, exercise yards, a playground and swimming pool for every dog, and state of the art whelping facility and puppy nursery for the Labradoodle girls and their litters. Before long I was receiving visits from veterinarians, academics and officials who were interested in the development of my new breed and impressed by the modern, clean and scenic parkland facilities where the dogs were kept beautifully groomed and cared for by a crew of full time dog loving staff members.

*Rutland Manor Entrance*

*Labradoodles playing in Rutland Manor Parklands*

*Puppies' Adventure Playground*

## DOODLE CRAZE HITS HOLLYWOOD

My vow to educate people about the new breed took on a whole new meaning after exporting my first Australian Labradoodle puppies to the United States in 1998. Media attention attracted intense interest and ignited the Australian Labradoodle frenzy in America which spread across the USA like wildfire. Labradoodles started turning up from one end of the country to the other, including in Hollywood where friends Sharon and Philip Steele created a stir on Rodeo Drive in Beverly Hills with 'Rutlands Princess Hana Doodle'.

*Rutlands Princess Hana Doodle on Rodeo Drive Beverly Hills California*

Little did I know that I 'hadn't seen nothin' yet'. When the Chicago Tribune published a full length article on Sunday October 21, 2001 it mentioned my visit to the US and featured some of the puppies that I had sent to American families. After this international media exposure my telephone ran hot with requests from newspapers and magazines in the United States, the UK, Japan and Europe asking for interviews about the amazing new dog breed from Australia that didn't shed, was allergy friendly and could read people's thoughts and emotions.

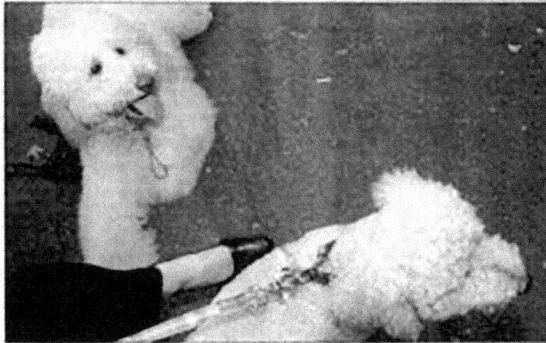

*Chicago Tribune October 21, 2001*

On January 18, 2004 the National Geographic featured the Australian Labradoodle in its television documentary entitled 'Designer Dogs' in which it devoted a fifteen minute segment to the developing breed's allergy friendliness, its Australian origin and the traits which made the breed unique. The National Geographic film crew traced the journey of a puppy from Rutland Manor Labradoodle Breeding and Research Centre in Australia to its arrival at O'Hare International airport in Chicago where a nervous young mother was waiting with her severely allergic seven year old son to pick up the puppy. Included in the filming, was a follow up segment four months later that showed the young boy deliriously happy with his puppy and free of any allergic reaction to it. Although the term 'designer dog' was incorrect when describing the Australian Labradoodle, since the term refers to offspring of different breeds or cross breeds, rather than the distinct pure breed that I was developing the National Geographic reporter Bijal Trivedi got it right in her February 9 article of the same year, when she wrote: 'the evolving Labradoodle had a purpose: to provide an allergy friendly companion, especially to people with special needs'. [14]

Before too long the phone at Rutland Manor was ringing day and night with calls from Europe, Canada and the United States. To my utter surprise, scores of people were so fascinated by my new breed that they traveled half way around the world especially to meet them. It was a heady and exciting time, and I loved welcoming my international visitors into my home and introducing them to the Labradoodles. When they were due to arrive, I raised their national flag up my flagpole alongside the host Australian flag, and my visitors were always touched and delighted by this gesture. Frequently I hosted open days and entertained in a marquee with gourmet food provided by caterers, since the sheer numbers of visitors now exceeded my ability to provide home cooking for all of them.

*Rutland Manor flying the flags*

*Marquee for the guests*

By now the breed was much more than a family pet, it was generating good will and raising bundles of money for charity.

In 2005 the Labradoodle made world headlines again when giant US retailer Maurices sold 50,000 limited edition plush toy Labradoodles through more than 500 of their national chain stores, with $2.0 0 of the net proceeds from each $5.00 toy donated to cancer research.[15] The following year the Labradoodle

sparked another massive donation of $55,000 to Guiding Eyes for the Blind, this time through Lloyd and Taylor, when the retailer featured cuddly toy Labradoodles in its holiday catalogue in all 54 of its stores located in 11 states throughout America. [16]

By 2006 the Australian Labradoodle was a household name in the United States, and after a popular poll had gathered 8.5 million votes, Parker Brothers, the makers of the Monopoly Board Game, replaced the Scottish Terrier on the new U.S. Monopoly board games with a Labradoodle player piece. [17]

The Australian Labradoodle had not failed to capture the attention of celebrities either, and after ensuring that they were not seeking a puppy as a status symbol or fashion accessory, I was happy to send puppies to some loving celebrity homes. That started a non stop round of celebrity enquiries for my puppies which included Barbara Eden of I dream of Jeannie fame. My first meeting with Barbara was hilarious. Not long after I provided her with a lovely Rutland Manor Chocolate Australian Labradoodle, which she called 'Djinn Djinn' (named after her invisible dog in the 'I Dream of Jeannie' television series), we both met up at a Doodle Romp in California. I was struck by her youthful beauty as she approached me with her lovely Djinn Djinn by her side, and I felt delighted and privileged to meet her in person. She beamed her gorgeous smile as she reached me, and we both said simultaneously: 'It is such an *honour* to meet you!' after which we both burst out laughing.

*Barbara Eden with Rutlands Djin Djin (Image courtesy of Marius Luppino)*

I bred another delightful dog for Tom Griswold of the hit radio program 'The Bob and Tom Show'. He was so in love with his Miniature Rutland Manor puppy 'Tazzie' that he wrote about him on the Bob and Tom website, and when I wondered why a million emails crashed my system I discovered that Tom had put my website URL up as well. I had to thank him but respectfully ask him to please remove it since my internet provider's server was at risk of permanently crashing. These were certainly heady days for me and for the new breed.

*Tom Griswold with Rutlands Tazzie*

The Labradoodle's huge popularity, however, was a two edged sword, since in one twelve month period alone, over 350 new breeders sprang up in the United States who were randomly crossing all sorts of breeds with Poodles. Before too long, there were thousands of oddly shaped, hair coated, and hyperactive puppies passed off as Labradoodles. When history seemed to be repeating itself I despaired, but by this time the internet was up and running and I had a website built and set up one of the first chat site to discuss the new breed. These tools enabled me spread the message more widely, and conscientious breeders surfaced, who were interested in maintaining the integrity, allergy friendliness and health of the developing original Australian Labradoodle breed. Some of them imported authentic breeding stock from Australia and began their own responsible breeding programs.

This surge in popularity led to the beginning of American 'Doodle Romps', the first of which was organised by Philip and Sharon Steele in the autumn of 2002. This inaugural event was held at their home in Southern California with an attendance of 40 people and 20 Labradoodles who all spent the afternoon swimming in the Steele's pool. From then on the number of guests escalated each year until the Southern California Doodle Romp was moved to the Steeles' tree studded Oak Grove property in Malibu. People traveled to California all the way from Arizona, Massachusetts, Mississippi, and from as far away as Hawaii to attend the romp, and when RSVP replies reached 400 in 2012 the hosts felt compelled to introduce a limit of 350 people and their dogs. The event was particularly popular since it featured a sumptuous buffet served with wine, where guests ate at tables covered with linen tablecloths topped with elegant flower decorations, in the tranquil setting of Oak Grove. Sharon calls the day 'Woodstock for dogs' because of its harmonious vibe, with hardly a bark heard from such a large number of dogs, many meeting for the first time, and all getting along well together (typical of the breed). This spectacular annual event has evolved into a major charity fundraiser, with a live auction, local television personalities, vendors selling any and all things dog related, and a number of contests open to all, which include obedience trials, and novelty events.

The Steele's beautiful Oak Grove property was also the venue, in September 2006, for the world's first conformation Breed Specialty Show for the Australian Labradoodle and I flew from Australia to California to judge it, with suitcases filled with beautiful prize sashes, rosettes and ribbons which I'd had made in Melbourne. I also donated thousands in cash prizes to the winners of the competitions. An impressive entry of 60 registered Australian Labradoodle dogs and puppies presented for judging and many others took part in the novelty events also run on the day.

*Ribbons for first Labradoodle Conformation Breed Show*

*Beverley Judging at Malibu*

These conformation shows went a long way toward protecting the new breed standards and preserving the attributes of the cuddly original Australian Labradoodle, but all worthwhile endeavors can have hazardous beginnings. As the authentic Labradoodle became even more popular, I was to encounter stormy weather from a number of fronts.

Within the next ten years I would experience massive betrayals and wholesale theft of dozens of my valuable dogs with irreplaceable bloodlines, perpetrated by envious breeders and vigilantes posing as animal liberationists who started hate sites to ruin my professional reputation. This harassment seemed almost unthinkable to me at first since most Labradoodle breeders in the world started out (and many continue) with my bloodlines, and since I was the co-founder and developer of the Australian Labradoodle in the first place. Worse still, the harassment came at a huge personal and professional cost and almost resulted in the extinction of the original and irreplaceable Australian Labradoodle bloodlines dating back to the very origins of the Labradoodle in the late 1980s.

Fortunately, however, this extinction didn't happen despite the most vile and persistent efforts of some very unscrupulous people and groups that cost me my property, my home and my savings. A more detailed overview of the destructive forces I had to contend with is provided by Tom Smith Esq. who was kind enough to write a foreword to this book entitled 'Introduction To Dog Politics' on page 9.

Without going into the unpleasant details of the malicious attacks, (this is for another book), I need to mention the reason that the original bloodlines from the Australian Labradoodle survived at all; it was purely because I had to protect, at all cost, a small core of dogs that carried the best of the original bloodlines. This meant that I had to move to a very remote area and endure some severe deprivations to prevent further assaults on me and my animals. But miraculously, out of such adversity, came a miracle. From that core of rare bloodlines that I had salvaged emerged what is now known as The Australian Cobberdog – a pure breed in development that is derived from the best and original genetics of the original Australian Labradoodle. This priceless and precious new breed has a strict breed standard that is now protected by an international dog registry. The strict enforcement of the breed standard should prevent the Cobberdog from going the way of the Australian Labradoodle at the hands of unscrupulous breeders. But before I elaborate more on the subject of breed standards in later chapters, I want to introduce the reader, without further ado, to the Australian Cobberdog. The next chapter gives the reader a taste of what it is like to own and train a puppy from this unique and loveable breed of dog, but it is not all beer and skittles!

# Kings and Queens of Jocks and Socks

L iving with an Australian Cobberdog can be a round of giggles, belly laughs, frustration, and moments of wonder and tender awe. In the early days when they were largely unknown other than by reputation, people always asked me if they were more like a Labrador or a Poodle. Apart from answering that they were like neither, having now evolved into a unique breed unto themselves, I hesitated to extol their virtues in case I appeared either biased, or inclined towards exaggeration. But as time went on the sheer volume of public opinion that sang the breed's praises gave me the confidence to share more fully about its amazing intuition and ease of training.

I felt incredibly validated when people told me that before I sent them their puppy, they'd thought that even if it was only half as good as I'd claimed, it would still be a great dog, yet it turned out to be so much better than they had expected. This kind of feedback soon became the norm, but it thrills me to this day when those emails still come rolling in. It's not easy to convey what makes these dogs so different from others without sounding like a besotted granny, and perhaps it mightn't even be possible to understand the Cobberdog's uniqueness unless you have actually met or lived with one, but I'll try.

Imagine a dog who is constantly seeking intimate eye contact with you. Wherever you are, inside your home, outside gardening, or on a walk, you are aware that this dog is one hundred percent tuned in to your inner self. You turn to look at him and his gaze is locked into yours, searching your feelings and thoughts. It would be lovely to think that your dog is tuning in to you for some noble purpose of his own and there are definitely many times when this is exactly what is happening with your Australian Cobberdog, but this goofy, fun loving clown also uses his intuitive ability to read your mind for less altruistic purposes. Although he will instinctively comfort you if you are sad or ill – for as long as it takes – he can also instantly transform into a fun-filled athlete, ready to play if you are in an active mood. He also knows when you are distracted, and with his wry sense of humour he will take full advantage of your lack of focus and either pull a playful stunt to gain your attention, or avoid doing what you have just asked.

A few years ago I sent a female puppy called Callie to a man who held a responsible position as head of a major hospital organization, and sometimes he hosted stately formal gatherings for influential colleagues in his home. One evening as a dozen or so guests were assembled in the dining room, his eighteen month old Cobberdog puppy came prancing down the staircase with one of his teenage daughter's bras dangling from her mouth and the red faced young girl was in hot pursuit. Callie trotted proudly around the room with her head held high and tail wagging as she darted in and out amongst the visitors' legs, obviously enjoying the ripples of laughter in the room, and being the centre of attention. With that first performance, however, the die was cast. From then on, whenever the family was entertaining, Callie would manage to find a bra or a pair of briefs from somewhere and give a repeat performance. Australian Cobberdogs are gatherers and empire builders; the kings and queens of jocks and socks. If you can't find some items in your laundry or cupboard, you're likely to come across them, without a mark or a tear, neatly piled like a treasure trove on your Cobberdog's bed.

Many people want to own an intelligent dog, but few realise the challenges that can come along with it. Just like smart kids, intelligent dogs have active minds that thrive on having something to think about. Leave a clever child in a room with nothing to do and you will soon have a frustrated and misbehaving child on your hands. Leave a smart dog to its own devices with no mental stimulation and no training and you can expect a whole host of unwanted behaviours; digging holes, pulling washing out of the clothesbasket, chewing things not made for chewing, jumping on people, barking or howling, and anything else that will catch your attention. For them, negative attention is better than none at all.

My wise old grandmother used to say 'the devil finds mischief for idle hands' and I would add to this: 'for idle paws too'. Australian Cobberdogs are very smart. What's more, they are convinced that they are people. They want human companionship and need to know that they belong as a valued member of the pack that consists of you and your family. I sometimes refer to them as 'Velcro dogs' because any time you look around, there they are, just a step or two behind you, wanting to be a part of whatever you are doing. Take a shower, and a couple of soulful eyes are watching over you. Go to the toilet and Fido will pad along with you and sit patiently watching your every move and maybe even try to help! Wherever you are, is where your Cobberdog wants to be. This is one of the traits that makes them such naturals as Assistance and Service Dogs, and as Medical Alert Dogs and Therapy Dogs, because they naturally focus on their humans and try to discern their mood and state of well-being. If you want a family companion, this attention could be either a wonderful experience or an annoyance, depending upon your own nature and circumstances. Personally, I find the dogs' undivided attention extraordinarily endearing and a great help in dog training. If you have the desire to learn to read the body language and facial expressions of your Australian Cobberdog and to recognise and work with his personality; it will fast track you to achieving the results you want from your dog training program.

Australian Cobberdogs are kid magnets. If your dog is not with you, and you're looking for him, just find the children. Remember those moments of wonder and tender awe I mentioned? Watch one of these dogs interacting with a young child and the sweet memory of it will forever linger in your heart.

Choosing the breed which will be the best fit for you and your family is a big decision that will determine the well-being of both humans and dog, and the very traits that may endear a particular breed to one person, may drive another to distraction. In this summary I am attempting to portray a balanced picture of the Australian Cobberdog as well as presenting you with a sense of what it would be like to live with one. Perhaps the following check list may help you decide if this is the dog breed for you.

1. Am I willing, and do I have the time to train my new puppy a few times a week for at least the first twelve months?

2. If I am inexperienced or run into a problem that I can't solve in my dog's best interests, am I prepared to engage the help of a professional dog trainer or dog psychologist?

3. Do I have the time to brush my dog's coat once a week and if not, do I have the resources to employ a professional groomer at least once a month?

4. Will my dog's constant companionship be irritating to me?

5. Am I prepared to accept my dog as a part of my family rather than an outside pet left to its own devices?

6.   Will I be able to accept, with humour, my dog's occasional displays of mischief, whilst administering firm guidelines for his behaviour?

If you have checked all the boxes, chances are you are the ideal candidate to own an Australian Cobberdog.

The Australian Cobberdog offers more to us than we could ever imagine, but puppies don't come with best behaviours already formed; he is a blank canvas, other than the sound genetic heritage behind him and the early socialising his breeder gave him. Like any dog, an untrained Australian Cobberdog can become attention seeking. Training requires consistent effort, especially for the first critical twelve months, and this will set him up for good behaviour for the rest of his life.

Did you know that you are already a dog trainer? Training animals has fascinated me since I was a child when I taught tricks to my school friends' dogs and ponies to earn pocket money. Good training is relevant to so many situations in our daily lives that I looked up its definition. The Wikipedia Free Dictionary defines it this way:

> *'Training is the acquisition of knowledge, skills, and competencies as a result of the teaching of vocational or practical skills and knowledge that relate to specific useful competencies...'*

When I think of training an animal, I define it as a meeting of minds between different species. Many years ago dog training meant issuing orders and forcing the dog to obey them. My instincts have always rebelled against this crude methodology, and during the 1980s when I instructed at Southern Obedience Dog Club in Melbourne, I was often figuratively rapped over the knuckles for not conforming to the training methods of the time. Dogs in general are exquisitely aware of human body language and I could never relate to the way handlers were taught to yell at their dogs. It jarred my every nerve and I refused to teach my students that way. I suspect the club would have sent me packing if they hadn't been so short of instructors. Fortunately, training methods have changed a lot from those days.

If you have a dog, then you are already a dog trainer, although you may not necessarily be aware of it. Your dog is reading you constantly, whenever he is in your presence, or even at a distance, whenever he can see you. He is watching you and observing your body language to work out how your mind ticks. To him this is very useful information and it determines how he responds to you in many different situations. You may notice that he is more obedient or responsive to certain members of your family than to others. This is because he has studied each of you, and knows how far he can push the limits and with whom, and most importantly he knows who is the pack leader.

The essence of your relationship with your Australian Cobberdog is defined by what he notices in your daily interactions with other people and with him. It is up to us to use this valuable knowledge to our best advantage. Awareness, consistency and repetition are the keys to successful training. For example, if you have asked your dog to do something that he is avoiding, and you fail to follow through, he will have you tagged as a softie and will exploit that inconsistency any chance he gets - purely for fun and just because he can!

A dog's physical responses are the outward expression of a thought which may be transmitted from your mind to his, and most dogs want to please you at all cost. In the early 1990s I learned from Michael Tucker, an Australian dog trainer and dog psychologist, the importance of thinking like a dog in order to communicate with one. Before Cesar Milan made dog psychology as popular as it is today, Michael was one of the original dog psychologists and when I attended one of his courses I was impressed with his training methods, which were based on the principle of mutual affection and respect. He had trained police dogs in the Royal Air Force, and spent twenty years training guide dogs for the blind in Australia and in the UK.

He was a fountain of knowledge gained from his extensive experience and his perspective made a lasting impression on me.

It's interesting how something very small can influence one's thinking. Mr Tucker shared a simple little story which occurred during his time working with Guide Dogs, but it gave me fresh insights. He told of a young Labrador who was doing its street training and was going very well, until it came to a certain place in the busy shopping area. Every day the young dog would baulk and refuse to cross one particular intersection. Michael told us that he thought it would be a pity to fail such a promising dog on this one issue, and he wanted to understand the dog's reason to fear this one specific place. He said that right there, in the middle of the busy thoroughfare, he knelt down on the pavement's edge beside the dog to see that intersection the way the dog was seeing it from its own height and perspective. From this angle, he saw the flashing signs of some road works barricades that were disturbing the dog. This enabled him to address and solve the problem by leading the dog from his other side until he became used to the lights and stopped reacting to them. The story concluded with the dog passing its training.

When I heard this, something clicked in my own mind, and since that day I have been keenly interested in learning as much as possible about the workings of a dog's mind and putting what I learn into practice. Dogs think in terms of cause and effect and they will want to repeat any action that brings pleasure or praise. Conversely, if something they do or think of doing results in pain or an unpleasant experience, they will not want to perform that action again. We should aim for our dogs to eagerly seek our will, with obvious enjoyment and confident anticipation of our happy approval.

A lot has been written in recent years about 'positive' or 'affirmation' training. But these terms are relative and open to different interpretations.

In my opinion, it is necessary to establish patterns of light and shade, and to set clear guidelines in 'dog language' to a young puppy, or adult dog in training. I believe that it is just as important to caution or correct when needed, as it is to praise when the dog shows the slightest *intention* of complying with our wishes. We should give encouraging praise at the precise moment the dog is *thinking* about responding the way we want, because that is the instant in which he will make his decision one way or the other. His intention will be in his eyes and body language before he makes his move, and when we learn to read him the same way he reads us, our training together will be truly a meeting of the minds. Clicker training helps many people to connect their timing with the dog's thought processes and actions.

Timing is crucial when giving correction or praise. A dog thinks in a series of snapshot seconds. I think of it in terms of a sequence of movie film frames. The first frame is the thought, the second frame is the decision and the third frame is the physical action that the thought has originated. It's far more effective to anticipate and avoid an inappropriate behaviour by cautioning the dog and following it by praise when he responds, than it is to wait too long and then punish the dog when the action has taken place and it's all over. By then the dog has forgotten about it and will perceive the discipline as a punishment.

I have known people who were convinced that their dog knew he'd done wrong many hours after the event. 'Oh yes, he knows, all right!' they'd say. 'As soon as I come home from work and he's torn the clothes off the clothesline, he creeps up to me on his belly so I tell him what a bad dog he is, but he just doesn't get it, he's so stubborn'. Poor dog, there are two serious flaws in this approach. Firstly, when the pack leader appears and sees the clothes on the ground, he feels irritation or even anger. His body language makes it plain to his dog that the leader is displeased, but since the event happened much earlier in the day the dog has no idea what he's done wrong. However, having a beautiful 'dog' nature, the dog cringes up begging forgiveness for the unknown misdemeanor. But what does he get for his trusting approach? A scolding! With this approach the owner has confused his dog, and taught him not to come when called as well.

I believe that dogs are neither 'good' nor 'bad', they have merely had their behaviour conditioned by their owners who find certain behaviours acceptable and others unacceptable. Everything depends on what your own family defines as appropriate behaviour. You may allow your dog to sleep on the furniture, while your neighbour may not. It is up to you to define your own house rules first, make sure each family member understands and will support you, and then gently but firmly go on to establish these rules in your own dog's mind until they become a habit. Clear guidelines need to be set and consistently re-enforced. It's unfair to let our dog leap all over us when we are in our old clothes, and then expect him not to jump on us when we are dressed to go out. He should be either allowed to jump up, or not be allowed to jump up – with no exceptions unless clearly invited to do so.

I like to address unwanted behaviour by the degree of difficulty needed to correct it. Each problem has a corresponding corrective tool which I measure by imagining its intensity in 'weight'. If one pound's weight of correction doesn't work, it is pointless to continue using one pound. Instead I try two pounds and so on. Each dog is an individual, with his own level of sensitivity. One size doesn't fit all, and all unwanted behaviours are not equal.

Puppies sometimes - no, make that often - know what you want, but they try you out to see if they can get away with not doing it. I don't see this as being stubborn or rebellious, but rather their way of establishing whether you are worthy of their respect and therefore a safe leader to follow. If they don't have confidence in you, then whether or not they want to, they will take the lead by default. It's just a dog's nature needing to know his place in the pack, so a young puppy especially follows his instinct and takes actions to help him work that out in his own mind. You are being tested!

By nature, dogs interact with one another in a very physical way. A mother dog will discipline her babies quite roughly at times if they take no notice of her earlier reprimands. If a warning growl (one pound) hasn't had any effect then she may snarl (two pounds). If she is still ignored, she may snap at the puppy (three pounds) or in an extreme case, pick it up by the scruff of the neck and shake it (four pounds). The erring puppy may yelp and run away, but it knows that she will always welcome it right back without holding a grudge, and will lick and reassure it the instant its unwanted behaviour stops. Humans have much to learn from dogs!

If it's cute for a little puppy to jump up for patting and loving, and not cute for the same puppy to do exactly that when it's grown up and 80 lbs then it isn't fair to give the signal of approval when it is little and expect it to understand when the goal posts are moved later on in life.

Even grown dogs instinctively want to know who is leader of any pack, because dogs are hard wired to be pack members, and survival in the wild depends on each animal knowing its place in the pecking order. All members of the pack look to the leader for direction and his position is usually gained or kept in the wild after fighting it out with an aspiring challenger wanting the top position. Deep within the domestic dog there still beats the heart of the wolf, and the only thing that has changed is that you and your family members are now, or should be, the leaders of your dog's pack. If you are not, then your dog will step into this leadership vacuum and take on this essential role by default.

The privilege of being pack leader doesn't come automatically. Every new puppy's instinct drives him to discover, by trial and error, whether he or another dog is leader of his pack. It is through training that we help our puppy to discover this all important knowledge. He already knows who was leader of his litter and he gained this information from all the tussling, fighting and growling that went on among his siblings as they fought over food, their mother's attention and coveted toys. Just when the puppy is confident and settled, he leaves his litter mates to come to your home, and finds himself in a strange place among a new pack. He will immediately want to know who is leader in this new environment and he tries to find out by using the same instinctual tactics as he did determining his litter's pecking order; by nipping, biting and challenging. At first his attempts may be tentative as he tests the waters, but if you do not make it clear that you are the leader, his challenges will increase in intensity and require firmer training techniques later on to get your message across.

Our voice is a valuable tool when we are training our puppy, not so much by the words we speak, but the tone in which we say them. When a puppy jumps up and nips or bites, the word 'no' by itself isn't going to mean much to that puppy, unless the tone is gruff and sounding like a growl, (dog language) or some other body language has illustrated to the puppy what the word means. I will first use 'uh uh' in a sharp tone because it's more of a warning than a reproof. It catches a puppy's attention and in that split second that he looks at me (focus being the first essential contact) I then have the opportunity to convey the message I want him to understand. The high pitched voices and rapid speech of children excite a puppy, whereas lower range softly spoken words tend to calm him. Puppies will often jump, nip and chase the kids when they don't do it to the adults in the household. But most of all, body language speaks loudly to all dogs and puppies.

Trainers of animals such as Liberty Horses understand the concept of body language and its powerful influence, which is why they can direct unbridled horses into any direction, and elicit specific actions from them at a distance and with no equipment other than a long whip (used only as an extension of their arm). Animals are sensitive to our body language and we can utilise this in our training. Understanding body language and animal psychology has helped me to train both dogs and horses without using coercive methods or gear. The next picture shows me demonstrating riding without a bridle on my Quarter Horse 'Yulgilbar Pablo' for the television program 'Talk to The Animals'. Pablo would turn in any direction that I inclined my head towards, and responded to my slightest body movements. I was in my fifties at the time and the strap was for me to hold onto, not to guide Pablo!

*Pablo and I rehearsing for a bridle-less riding demonstration
at the 'Talk to the Animals' Expo held at Caulfield
Racecourse in Melbourne Australia, in 1993*

Years ago I had my own mobile dog training service, and went to the dogs' own homes for the training sessions. People usually waited until their dog was fully grown and totally out of control before they called me, so I had some pretty tough customers. When I had a 90 lb monster pulling my arm out of its sockets on the leash, I sometimes had to physically rein them in to gain initial control, and occasionally the owner's face showed surprise because I had consistently emphasized gentleness. But once the animal knew that I could speak his language, he had no problem following my directions and the owners were always surprised (I wasn't) when their dog behaved perfectly for me and wanted to go with me when I left. The dogs gazed at me with absolute adoration, totally ignored their doting owners, and greeted me with great excitement on my next visit. Did they love me more than they loved their owners? Not at all, but they were so relieved that they finally knew their place and had a leader to follow that they wanted to be in the reassuring presence of a pack leader.

In case you have not made it clear that you are the pack leader, I have compiled a list of some of the ways we can help our new puppy or an older dog to understand his rightful place in his human pack.

1.   Feed ourselves first and let the puppy watch us eating. If necessary, tether him just out of reach of our table. Leader of the pack, in the puppy's mind, is the one who gets to eat first. We don't give him scraps from our table and we pay no attention to him while we eat, other than a warning 'uh uh' and looking away, if he jumps up to the table. If necessary we can raise an elbow which presents a physical and emotional barrier, but we do not look at him, or touch him. We are merely exercising our right, as leaders of the pack, to get our food first and after a couple of unsuccessful attempts to intrude, he will quickly understand.

2.   We always walk through a door or a gateway first, and then invite the puppy to follow. This is best taught on the leash. Words like 'wait' or 'go back' will help to re-enforce the backward tugs on the puppy's leash, and an upright raised hand, palm facing him (like a STOP signal). When we are ready, and only then, can he be invited by using a release word ('come') and we should always praise him when he comes. If he thinks about breaking through but hasn't done so yet, I use the cautionary 'uh uh' in a warning voice and repeat the 'wait' request. I find the tone and intent which that short and sharp 'uh uh' term conveys can really help persuade a dog to

change its mind. Once this lesson is learned, the leash will not be needed and as we approach a doorway or a gate in the future, all we'll need to do is remind him with a verbal 'wait' command before we walk through ourselves.

3.  When we take our puppy out in the car, we should walk him on a leash and have him sit while we open the car door. If he goes ahead and jumps in before we invite him with our chosen word, we close the door again and put the puppy back into the sit position. This is repeated until the puppy remains in the sit position and we can release him to jump into the car. The reverse applies when we let him out of the car again.

4.  A common problem that many people experience when they take their dog to the dog park, is that when it's time to go home, the dog is having so much fun that he won't want to come when he's called, because he knows he's going to be taken away from his 'friends' and play time is over. If this happens more than once, it can undo weeks of recall training and you may lose your dog's respect the more he gets away with refusing to come to you right away when you call. My solution to this problem is to leave the dog on leash for the first ten minutes after we enter the dog park. I play tug toy games with him and treat him a few times. Just before I treat him, I call him by name and say 'come'. When I have his full attention and he is eagerly anticipating the treats, I take off the leash. Before I let him race off to play, I call him to me another two or three times, and pet and treat him. During his play time with the other dogs, I occasionally call him to me and give him another treat, but without touching him. I continue to do this a few more times, progressing to holding his collar and patting him while I treat him. This confuses him, because he doesn't know whether I'm calling him to offer him a

treat, or whether we are going home. I've never known a dog that doesn't respond to this method.

5. Dogs naturally understand seniority. If we have other dogs, we should always treat or feed them in order of their seniority and with the newcomer puppy last. This re-enforces the seniors' place of privilege in the pack as well as avoids jealousy, and a new puppy will understand that he is the lowest pack member among both humans and the other dogs as well. This natural order will keep harmony among the dogs.

The Australian Cobberdog puppy yearns to please and soaks up education like a sponge, especially during its first twelve months of life. The more he is asked to learn, the happier and more contented he is. Puppies of this breed are highly intelligent and will usually pick up on an instruction in just one lesson, but we need to be sure he understands it before we pass on to the next exercise. For instance, if we are teaching the puppy to automatically sit every time we stop walking, it would not be wise to teach or practice the 'drop' or 'lie down' in the same training session.

The old saying that prevention is better than cure is my motto when training a puppy or an older dog, and this breed's expressive body language and eye expression gives every opportunity to an intuitive trainer to alter and re- direct the intention or thought taking place in the dog's mind before it develops into unwanted action.

If we are alert, we will pick up signals from our puppy that forewarn us of what he's thinking about doing next. Suppose we are out walking and a strange cat darts into view. The puppy's first instinct may be to chase it, but before he does, his body language will show what he is thinking. The first signal will be a slight stiffening of his body and tail, which he may raise, or he may tremble with excitement. His gaze will be fixed on the cat and he may hold this posture for several seconds before he launches off in the cat's direction. These valuable seconds give us the opportunity to interrupt his thought pattern with decisive action. A good way to handle this situation would be to caution him first, with the 'uh uh' or 'leave it' and then supplement this with short tug and release of your leash if the verbal warning hasn't caught his attention.

The *instant* that he looks at you, it is very important to enthusiastically praise him. Then I suggest that you engage him in something fun, like a game of tug toy, and at the same time turn away from the object of his fascination. If his focus leaves you though, repeat the caution; 'uh uh'. If that does not deter him, you can add in a more forbidding growling tone add – 'aaahhhhhh', 'no chase' or 'leave it!' On the other hand, if he doesn't look at you and refuses to take his eyes off whatever has caught his attention, then it's time to distract him in a more motivating way such as walking around him to the left in a tight circle or reminding him to 'heel' with voice and leash commands, until he finally sits down because you're going nowhere (time to praise).

Learning to read a puppy's body language can be a challenge when we are caught up with how adorable he is! Every expression, including the mischievous ones, can be so darned cute. But it is well worth the effort to learn our dog's psychology, and the more we do, the easier and more natural it will become to read his every thought and behaviour.

There are times when we might think our dog is being disobedient or stubborn when he isn't responding to our requests. But his hesitation can have many causes, and accordingly, there are different ways to resolve the situation. We need to get into the habit of asking ourselves 'why', especially since Australian Cobberdogs are deep thinkers. There may be times when your dog just sits and looks at you when you have asked for a particular action. It's a good thing to give him the benefit of the doubt before you decide that he's being stubborn. He may be pondering over your request, and trying to understand what you mean. In this instance, an encouraging word, and a neutral repetition of the request may be all that's needed. It's also possible that he may have understood, but is thinking about whether or not he will obey, in which case the same repetition from you is appropriate.

With some exercises, such as calling him to you, your Australian Cobberdog puppy might try to run off, purely for the fun of enticing you into chasing him! His laughing expression will be a dead give-away. If this happens, and provided you are in a safe place, I suggest turning your back and walking briskly away without looking back. They hate to be ignored. When he runs to catch up with you, as he is bound to do, it's a good idea to play a cheerful game with him, touch him when you have the chance, hold his collar, tell him what a good boy he is - and then let him go free again (this is important so he forms a positive association with the exercise). This recall is best taught while the puppy is still very young. His every instinct tells him to come to you and to follow you. If I am working with a young puppy who I think is a little bit too independent, I start off with a long light cord attached to his collar. This gives me a better chance to stop him running off and I'm in a better position to guide him back to me, where of course I praise him and make a huge fuss about what a clever boy he is! Practice the recall from a short distance at first and gradually increase it as he gets better at coming to you. Habits learned at a young age tend to stick and the recall could one day save the dog's life if he will reliably return to your side in any situation.

Another method I use with an independent natured puppy is to carry a small tin with some pebbles in it in my pocket or treat bag. If the puppy ignores my call, I toss the tin so that it lands a little bit to the side and just in front of him. The noise of the rattling tin landing near him startles him just enough to momentarily break his concentration on what he is sniffing at or thinking about and that short few seconds gives me time to regain his focus. In the split second after the rattling tin catches his attention, I ask him to 'come' in an inviting voice and reel him in on the cord using short tugs. When he reaches me, whether happily or reluctantly, I play an exciting game of tug toy, ruff him up playfully a little bit and treat him. It is important that when he finally comes, it is an enjoyable experience, regardless of how naughty he has just been. A sharp clap of my hands and a high pitched yelp can help too, if I haven't got my pebble tin with me.

Puppies are cute, adorable and irresistible. But they soon grow up to be adult dogs and what they have learned when they were very young and impressionable tends to stay with them for life. If we pet and cuddle our new puppy when he stands on his hind legs, then it's teaching him that standing up on his back legs is acceptable behaviour. This soon turns into jumping up and not many people I know like dogs jumping on them and their friends and visitors. When a puppy jumps up to reach me for a cuddle, I put both hands around his shoulders, speak to him and gently put him in the sit position. This is my 'four paws on the floor' rule. I never pat my puppies if they are standing on their back legs for attention. Once their four paws are on the floor then and only then do they get the attention and petting that they're looking for. It's also important to use the same word every time he is placed back on the floor onto his bottom. It could be 'off' or 'down' but whatever word is used, it must always be the same one that will be used later on if he forgets and jumps up. Again, after your puppy obeys, immediate praise is very important.

Personally, I don't like to see someone push a puppy's hind end down when teaching him to sit. The method I find easiest and the most quickly effective for a puppy between eight and twelve weeks old, is to hold a small treat immediately above his nose, ask him to 'sit' and then move the treat back just out of his range. As he looks up and backwards at my hand, he will almost always automatically sit. If this doesn't work right away, I grasp him under the chin and elevate his head up and back until his bottom lands on the floor. The instant it does, I praise and treat. This method easily morphs to a simple raised forefinger 'sit' signal when the puppy is still at a distance. If we rely on physical pressure on the puppy's rump, we won't have the same measure of control, and applying hard pressure on a young puppy's rear end may even cause damage to his hip joints.

In a nutshell, I use six cardinal rules for training dogs or puppies.

1. I use the tone of voice which exemplifies the kind of message I want to convey to the dog. If I want to calm him, I use a soothing low voice. If I want to excite him, then I speak more quickly, and use a higher pitched voice and an excited tone.

2. Babbling is a definite no-no! I keep my sentences short and consistently use the same words that I want to imprint into the dog's mind relative to the task being taught.

3. Yelling is neither necessary nor helpful (unless the dog is a distance away).

4. Give the dog time to obey before repeating the request. I've come across dogs who thought that they should wait for 'sit' to be said five or six times before they are required to sit. This is easily fixed. After the second request, re-enforce with the leash, voice or hand signal, and expect a quick response this time.

5. Never train a dog or puppy when in a bad mood or in a hurry.

6. Ten minutes of daily training is better than an hour three times a week.

Above all, training should be fun for both you and your puppy. Who doesn't want to engage in a fun activity together? With a small amount of common sense training, your Australian Cobberdog will be your most loyal and perfect companion.

# Maintaining Their Natural Beauty

T he Australian Cobberdog has an eye catching silky fleece or wool coat that attracts attention wherever he goes. Owners often ask me for cards that they wish to hand out to the many admirers who pull them up in public places to ask what kind of dog it is, and where they can get one. This chapter will give you all the information you need to keep your Cobberdog in excellent trim and looking terrific.

## COAT

Most puppies have a baby coat which may be a different colour than it will be when the dog is mature. For example, a Dalmatian is born without spots, and a golden sable Scotch Collie (Lassie dog) puppy is covered in a rabbit grey fluff for the first few months of life. Shedding dogs such as these release their puppy coats when it's time for their adult coat to come through, and they continue shedding to various degrees throughout their lives. When I was breeding and raising German Shepherd dogs I rarely put away the vacuum cleaner for 31 years. This is not the case with Labradoodles, but I should warn the reader right up front that not all Labradoodles have non-shedding coats, there are many 'Labradoodle's around that are simply Labrador and Poodle crosses with inconsistent coats that shed and may not be allergy friendly. Unless otherwise specified, this book attributes these breed standard qualities only to the authentic Australian Labradoodle and the Australian Cobberdog which has been especially bred to have a single coat (meaning it has no fluffy undercoat) and it is reliably non-shedding and allergy friendly whether it is wool or fleece.

This also means that the authentic Australian Labradoodles i.e. Cobberdogs don't shed and are completely different from most other breeds. The upside is that there are no stray hairs coating your floors and carpets, or floating around the air and sticking to your clothes and furniture, and there is no doggy odour. The downside is that because the puppy coat will not shed out of its own accord, it needs to be stripped out, using a strong slicker brush, for the duration of the transition from puppy coat to adult coat, which could last from the time your puppy is about ten months old to one year or longer. If this is not done regularly, the old puppy coat twists into the new adult coat which is trying to push its way through, and this results in matting.

I think that the reason some dogs' coats are neglected, may be because they are difficult to groom or have very thick coats. One of the reasons that dogs can be afraid of the brush is that care hasn't been taken to avoid the sensitive dew claw area on the inside of the front ankle. When I'm brushing the front legs, I place my thumb over this area, which gives the dog confidence that I will not hurt him. It's easy for the unaware to miss what is happening with their dogs' coats, because matting starts close to the skin, and isn't immediately visible when the dog is brushed only across the surface. At first glance, everything appears to be just fine and beautiful, but when the coat is parted, the spreading lacework of matting can be seen hiding underneath. This is why it is so important to brush a small section at a time, layer by layer.

During the transition from puppy to adult coat, it helps to brush in several different directions; up, down and across, because when the coat is long, the strands are getting caught up together from different areas. The pictures featured next show how to hold up the top layers of the coat with one hand, while you brush a few hairs at a time down with the brush.

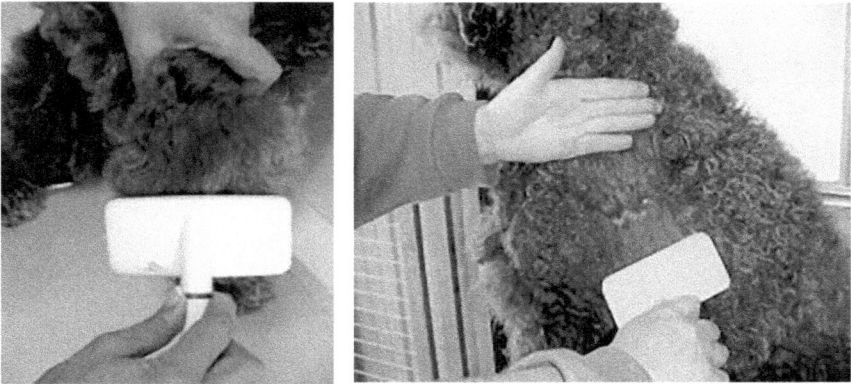

*Holding the top coat and brushing down in layers*

## TRIMMING AND CLIPPING THE FACE

I scissor trim around the Australian Cobberdog's face from time to time or his lush coat will grow profusely until it falls down over his eyes, which will hinder his vision and may, in time, even damage his eyes. As he matures, he will grow a long beard which should be trimmed short to prevent it from clogging with food and water, and to balance his face, I also trim the long coat that grows from his cheeks. I've always thought a neatly trimmed face is much cuddlier than a wet shaggy one!

Prepare for trimming by brushing first. This makes it easier to do a nice neat job with the scissors. The effect you are aiming for is a face that looks like the ruffled petals of a Chrysanthemum.

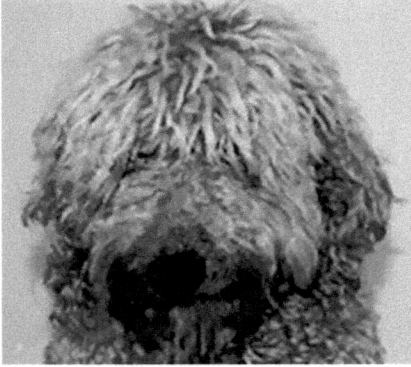

*Face before trimming*          *Same face after trimming and shaping*

## PAWS

I clip the top and undersides of the paws and around the edges a couple of times each year, using electric clippers and a size 15 blade. Scissors can be used instead of clippers, but don't do as neat a job. If the paws are not trimmed or clipped, the lower leg and foot coat will get shaggy and grow into what I call 'moccasins' which will collect sticks, dirt and other debris that the dog will tramp through the house. Moccasins will get wet, even from a quick trip outside for a potty break on a dewy morning, and they take a long time to dry, so it's better to have the feet coat trimmed short and the ankle coat trimmed just above ground level.

When I'm clipping or trimming the feet I hold up the long leg-coat with one hand while I trim, so that I leave enough length to drape down to ground level and cover the clipped area of the paws when I'm done. The ankles should not be showing.

*Overgown Moccasins*

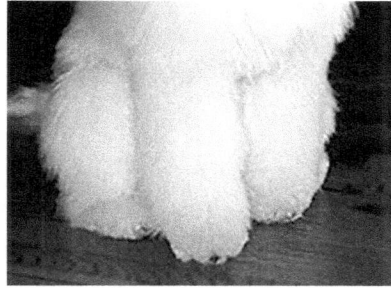

*Paws correctly trimmed*

## CUTTING THE TOENAILS

I give this only a brief mention here, because I recommend personal instruction in this very important aspect of caring for any dog's feet. A dog's toenails are shaped in an arc with the top two thirds being sensitive living tissue; much the same as the quicks of our own finger nails and toenails. Nature wants the quick to stay the same distance from the tip of the nail, so as the nail grows longer, the quick gets closer to the tip. Each time the end of the nail is clipped, the quick shrinks back the same distance further up the nail. If the nails have been allowed to grow very long, only a tiny section can be cut at a time, approximately each two weeks until the nail is the right length for comfort, i.e. not touching the ground.

Dogs have an 'extra' nail which often gets missed by pet owners, because it is higher up on the inside of the front ankles, attached to the 'dewclaw', a fleshy appendage with nail attached. Since this nail has no contact with the ground, it gets no wear. If it is not cut along with the others, it can grow into a circle and pierce the skin, necessitating surgical removal. Clipping a dog's nails may sound complicated, but it is easy once you have been physically shown how to do it by an expert. I recommend professional instruction before you attempt it yourself, because until you understand the technique it is easy to accidentally cut the blood vessel which is painful for the dog and distressing for you, when you see the blood oozing out from your dog's nail.

## LOOKING AFTER THE EARS

Many dog breeds with long pendulous ears are naturally prone to yeast ear infections. Prior to the infusion of the Irish Soft Coated Wheaten chronic ear infections were common in the Australian Labradoodle, but if your own dog doesn't carry this infusion, or your breeder has re-introduced Poodle into their Labradoodle breeding program, your dog may still have this problem. Either way, all dogs' ears should be cleaned regularly with one of the many good ear cleaning solutions on the market. A handy home-made maintenance treatment is a mix of 60% vinegar and 40 % water, or clinical alcohol. Saturate a cotton ball in the mixture, squeeze out the excess and wipe inside the ears, taking care to reach down deep into the crevices and being careful not to go too deeply into the ear canal. Use a fresh swab to dip into the solution each time in the same cleaning session. If there are any red or inflamed areas, use a commercial product available from your vet especially for the purpose, as the vinegar or alcohol will sting.

If your dog is scratching at his ears, and he doesn't have an infection, fleas or matted hair may be irritating him, or he may have ear mites, which are contagious and could have been picked up at the dog park, or when playing with someone else's pet. This will require a trip to the vet for an examination and specific treatment. Some dogs have thick hair growing inside their ears. These should be plucked out using your finger and thumb, or a pair of tweezers. Take only a few hairs at a time with a short sharp tug and he won't mind at all, and will enjoy a good hand rub and massage around his ears afterwards.

## BATHING

The Australian Cobberdog's coat naturally repels dirt and staining and if bathed too often, a self-perpetuating cycle is set up. In other words, the more often they are bathed, the more often they need to be bathed, because shampoos strip the coat fibres of their protective coating which stops the absorption of dirt (and the doggy odour that occurs in other dog breeds with hair coats).

A useful tip, if your Australian Cobberdog rolls in mud or dirt, is to sprinkle talcum powder (body powder) generously through the coat and leave the dog to dry naturally. The powder soaks up the dirt and smell and when it is dry and brushed out, the dog is as fresh and clean smelling as if he has just had a bath. Even light coloured dogs dry spotlessly clean when this method is used. It may be difficult to believe until you see it for yourself, but it works!

If you decide that your Australian Cobberdog does need a bath there are a few rules that will help achieve a successful outcome.

1. Brush him all over before wetting the coat. If there are tangles and knots underneath, wetting them will set the knots into mats that are as hard as acorns that are impossible to get out.
2. Plug the dog's ears with cotton wool before bathing, and remember to take the cotton wool out afterwards. Water in the deep ear canal can cause infections and as well as that, is the main reason so many dogs hate to be bathed, even though they love to swim!
3. Start by thoroughly wetting the neck all the way around and the chest. If there are any fleas on the dog, this will prevent them from getting into his ears as they try to escape the water.
4. Leave the head and face until last. Another reason that so many dogs don't like to be bathed is because they hate their faces to be wet for as long as it takes to bath and rinse the rest of them.

5. Squeeze the shampoo downwards through the coat with your fingers. Rinse and towel dry the same way. Don't scrub in circles. This is a sure way to tangle the coat which makes for a lot of work getting the knots out later. Some coat conditioners need to be rinsed out and others can be left in. Check the label. Rinse and squeeze excess water from the coat with a towel so as not to tangle the coat.

6. If you blow dry your dog, take the dryer in one hand and the brush in the other. Work on a small section at a time, blowing directly onto the area you are brushing layer by layer. There are several coat conditioning sprays and creams which can be applied and are designed to shorten the time needed for blow drying.

7. After the coat has been blown dry, it will be puffed up and very fluffy. A misting of water from a bottle will help the pretty tendrils to settle more quickly.

When brushing, trimming, or clipping, I find it much easier to manage the dog when he is up off the ground, on a table or bench, preferably in a corner of the room. A non-slipping surface, such as rubber matting, will give the dog confidence and help him to be co-operative when you ask him to lift a paw, for instance. If the grooming experience is pleasurable for him, it will be enjoyable for you as well.

Puppies should be groomed from early on, whether they need it or not, to accustom them to being quietly handled so that when they're older, it will be habit to allow every part of their body including legs, feet, tail and face to be handled and brushed or combed. I like to teach a puppy to lie down on the table for grooming, as well as to stand up. This makes it easier to reach some of the more inaccessible areas, gives him a rest from standing in the one place, and also helps to prevent bad habits like jumping down from the table while you aren't watching. Some dogs or puppies resist lying down to be groomed, and I will shortly describe a very successful technique that relaxes a dog completely while grooming. Invariably when I demonstrate it, some folk are so impressed that they think I have some mystical power, but this isn't so. Almost anyone can learn how to do it.

There are three major reasons for a dog to refuse to co-operate in a grooming session, and these may be: fear of being hurt, excitability, and or aggression, which can also be fear-induced. When I devised the calming technique that I am sharing in this chapter, the tools I used were based on the principle that I believe a dog's mind is in a Beta brain wave state when he is anxious or resisting. He just wants out of there, by any means possible. In the Beta state his mind is sharp and alert. He is totally focused on his own responses to stimuli, neurons are firing in rapid succession in his brain, and he will be able to move with lightning speed, to either escape, or if flight is prevented, to bite. While in this state of mind it will not be possible to reach him mentally or to positively influence him.

In order to connect with a resisting dog's mind, my first goal is to change his state of mind, and provided my own mind is in a peaceful place at the time, I will hopefully help him to transition from Beta's acute brain activity to the gentle Alpha brain waves of greater relaxation. I have noticed over the years, that in this state he will experience a liberating sense of peace and well-being where his fear will vanish. That done, I take the further step of helping him to enter the deeper relaxation of Theta brain waves, which neuroscience has identified as the gateway to learning, memory and deep relaxation. When we learn to achieve this relaxed state in our dog, it is important to provide only positive stimuli since the lessons he learns on the grooming table will stay with him for life. In my opinion, dogs usually don't block their progression into the Theta state, and the long, slow, undulating brain wave frequencies have restorative power to heal  previously held fears and mind attitudes.

I must stress that I have no scientific evidence to support the theory behind my technique, which I will shortly describe, and I have never heard of this psychological tool being used by others for dog training. But after using this technique on hundreds of dogs, often in public exhibitions, I have demonstrated conclusively how effective this relaxation technique can be.

The next series of pictures were taken during a grooming demonstration I did in Melbourne. I had asked for 'problem' dogs, and the first one brought to me was a silver haired dog called Tashi who attacked the brush each time his owner tried to groom him. The second was Bailey, a 12 month old caramel puppy that wouldn't let his owner anywhere near him with a brush. She told me that after he came back home from his first visit to a grooming salon, the very sight of a brush set him growling and snapping at her and now she was frightened to try and groom him. As she placed Bailey onto the grooming table in front of me, he clearly expressed fear of the brushes and combs, so the first thing I needed to do was to reassure him that he would not be hurt.

When Bailey's owner stepped away, all I did for a few minutes was to hold him close and breathe love and peace into him. When I felt his body relax, and only then, was it time to progress to the lesson. I always remove the collar and have no leash on a dog when I use this method. He then realises that I am not relying on restraint, and this prepares him for the relaxed state of mind that I am working towards.

*Relaxing Bailey before grooming*

To avoid emotional confrontation, I next needed to place Bailey into a situation which didn't remind him of the wins he'd had when he'd snarled at his owner and frightened her. When she told me that she had never tried to lie him down on the grooming table, this was the obvious place to begin. To illustrate the technique that I use to lie a reluctant dog down on the grooming table, I have used photographs of Tashi because they show my method more clearly. The other images are of Bailey.

## Step 1

My arms are wrapped around the dog, holding him close to my own body and with my face turned away. This is one of the rare occasions when we do not want the dog's focus or eye contact. We are looking for relaxation and calmness. If he struggles, we ignore this and continue to hold him firmly, with all his weight still on his four feet planted on the table. If we are calm, and our mind is in a peaceful state, it will take only between twenty and thirty seconds for the dog to flop in our arms like a rag doll.

*Step one*

## Step 2

When the dog is perfectly relaxed in my arms, and only then, do I step backwards away from the table, still hugging the dog. This moves his legs and feet off the table and positions him correctly so that when I step forwards again, it is easy to lean over him and lay him down on his side on the table. If he tenses, I stay in position leaning closely over him, and repeat in a low rhythmic voice: 'lie down, lie down, lie down, gooooooood boy; lie down, lie down'.

*Step two*

## Step 3

If he is thinking of jumping up, the first parts of his body to move will be his head, and the hind leg underneath. Maintaining my own relaxed state, I keep an eye on these and at the first sign of movement, I gently press them back onto the table and lean closely over the dog again, continuing to ask him to lie down. A useful way to take his mind off trying to get up again is to gently rub his tummy, all the while telling him to lie down and that he is a 'gooooood boy'. This phase of the exercise usually takes two or three minutes.

*Step three - fully relaxed*

Now the dog is fully relaxed and can be groomed without any resistance. When this occurs, usually within five short minutes, the onlookers are usually amazed and I often walk away from the table to show that the dog is there of his own accord after he has placed his complete trust in me and accepted me as his pack leader.

In this case, Tashi's owner is astonished as she watches me grooming him without protest after he would not allow her to brush even his tail. When I'd finished with Tashi, I repeated the technique with Bailey who was content to let me brush him from face to tail and to scissor trim his coat short with no incident, and with the formerly dreaded brush lying right in front of his nose. Bailey remains completely relaxed and is not distracted by another dog jumping up around the table next to him. He stayed deeply relaxed while I trimmed his beautiful light caramel coat. The test came when Bailey's owner picked up the brush and easily groomed him herself. She was ecstatic.

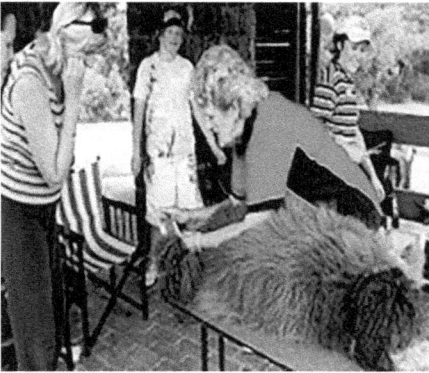

*Tashi's owner looking astonished*

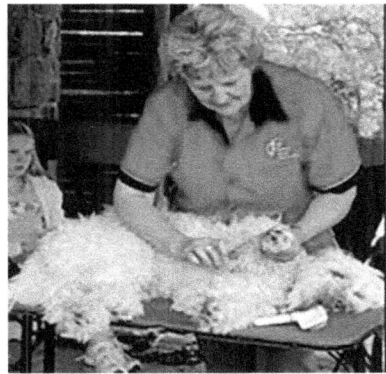

*Grooming a relaxed Bailey*

*Bailey relaxes despite other dog jumping up*

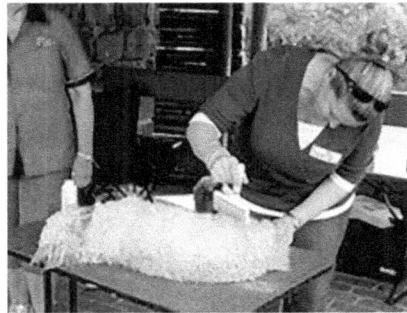

*Ecstatic owner grooms Bailey*

# HEALTH AND BEAUTY ON THE INSIDE DIET

Any discussion about beauty on the inside wouldn't be complete without mentioning a dog's inner health from a physical and biological perspective. Just as we feed our dog's mind and spirit through our bond with him, we also need to think carefully about the way we feed his body - the vessel that he uses to carry him around, to express his personality, his joy for living and his love and loyalty for us. By providing him with the best nutrition, we hope to keep him with us and in robust health for as many years as possible.

There are many things that contribute to inner health. I picture the living tissues, organs, blood vessels, and a myriad of naturally occurring bodily chemical reactions all working together in synchronous harmony. This depends entirely on optimal nutrition at the cellular level, but that is not as easily achieved as it sounds. I have long believed that many highly processed commercially prepared dog foods are no more beneficial to dogs than fast food and pre-packaged foods are for human beings. We can live on these 'foods' and grow fat, yet be starving for the essential nutrients at the same time. I grew up in an era when commercial dog foods were not yet invented. Dogs ate a wholesome varied diet of various fresh foods topped up with kitchen scraps, fresh meaty bones and table leftovers. Not only were life-style diseases in dogs unheard of, but veterinary clinics were not busy places crammed with ailing animals, as they are today.

Many years ago, when I first started breeding dogs, if anyone had prophesied that one day dogs would have to be anaesthetised to have their teeth cleaned, or that owners would brush their dogs' teeth with doggy tooth brushes, they would have been laughed off the planet – as would have been the case if anyone had foretold a time when dogs in huge numbers would suffer from allergies, sensitive stomach, numerous immune diseases and diabetes. Yet all this has come to pass, and is exponentially on the rise in the 21ˢᵗ Century. This tragic trend may slowly abate over time, as some pet food companies are working with recent research findings in the study of nutrigenomics. And if this awareness combines with public demand for more wholesome nutrition for our pets, perhaps this will bring about positive change in the way many commercial foods are processed and an improvement in the quality of their ingredients.

Nutrigenomics is the study of the way that food and genetics interact and Dr Jean Dodds is a leader in this research. As a veterinary scientist and renowned animal health expert, she has, for many years, studied nutrigenomics, the effects of nutrients and food constituents on gene expression. She notes the following in one of her many scientific papers:

*'Food components interact at the level of the genome, where they act by "up-or down-regulating" target genes. Different diets elicit different patterns of gene and protein expression...On this basis, diets for animals should be designed and tailored to the genome or genomic profile of individuals in order to optimize physiological homeostasis, disease prevention and treatment, and productive, athletic, obedience or reproductive performances. This approach individualizes dietary intervention to prevent, mitigate or cure chronic diseases.'* [18]

My take on Dr Dodd's work is that a poor diet can turn on genes that express illness while an appropriate diet can prevent 'bad' genes from being expressed while enhancing peak health and performance in the animal. I hope that this research will also lead to reversing the effects of multi generational health deterioration in all breeds of dogs due to being fed poor diets. Other research from Dr Dodds shows that many dogs have developed hidden sensitivities to various foods which in turn cause illness. Dr Dodds has developed NutriScan, a simple test to find out if your dog has food sensitivities. For the first time, dog owners can have the necessary information to be able to feed their dog an appropriate diet while avoiding the specific foods that cause their dog's symptoms, such as scratching from skin allergies. [19]

Personally, I am excited that science has now shown what many experienced dog breeders have already known; that your dog can be cured of various chronic illnesses by simply adjusting the ingredients of his diet. Over my 50 year career in dog breeding I have demonstrated time and again that a top diet consisting of fresh raw meat *with fat*, fresh raw chicken (with bones) fish, eggs, cheese, a few drops of cold pressed flax seed oil two or three times a week, a small quantity of green leafy vegetables and minimal to no along with soft raw meaty bones from young cattle or lambs, keeps dogs robustly healthy. Even more exciting for me has been watching hundreds of previously sick dogs restored to physical and mental health after their owners switched them to a nutrient rich diet.

## INTUITION

I have deliberately set out to develop bloodlines that produce dogs with obvious intelligence, gentleness and intuitive capacity. Many people have noticed this in the Australian Cobberdog and have described this as their 'inner beauty'. This precious state of being can be either nurtured and strengthened, or smothered and destroyed, by the ways in which his family interacts with him. If his natural intuition is recognised and encouraged, and if his active mind is stimulated through learning, he will have the best opportunity to reach his full potential. The dog is the sum total of his inner and outer experiences and environment. When he is a whole, happy and contented member of his human pack, he is capable of real initiative and incredible courage.

I once had a beautiful puppy that was inexplicably difficult to place in a suitable home. Melba had been allocated to a family, but they deferred to the next litter due to family circumstances. Two other people in a row deferred on her, while her siblings went off to their new homes, leaving her behind. As I watched this gorgeous, but still unplaced, puppy getting older, it just didn't make sense to me. There had to be a reason, but I couldn't figure out what it could be. Then one day an email came in from a lady in New York. Jackie wrote that she had been on my website just out of interest; not really looking for a puppy, when she saw Melba's photo. Something about the expression in this puppy's eyes spoke to her and she said that she just 'knew' that this puppy was meant for her and her family, although she didn't really know why.

Twelve months later another email arrived from Jackie with an astonishing account of how Melba had just saved the life of her youngest daughter, almost four years old. The older children were in the deep end of the swimming pool one afternoon, while their little sister was splashing about in the toddler's shallow end. Melba had shown no interest in the pool up to that time and was lying snoozing on the decking. Both parents had left the pool for only a few moments when they heard Melba barking. They hurried back to see their little girl struggling in the deep water, with the older children nowhere to be seen. Melba was racing frantically around the edge of the swimming pool, all the while yelping and barking. Before the parents could get through the well secured poolside fence, 15 month old Melba had already launched herself into the pool, grabbed the child's bathers in her teeth and towed her to the steps of the pool into her parents' arms. Melba had been raised as a true family member and even at such a young age, she had demonstrated initiative, loyalty and an intuitive awareness of what to do in a dangerous situation.

A lot of dog lovers smother-love their dogs with cuddles and kisses, and pamper them with plenty of new toys, matching collar and leash sets, expensive comfy beds to sleep on, and lots of treats on a daily basis.

I love to kiss and cuddle my dogs too, but I have found that those who also nurture and stimulate their dogs' higher mental attributes through training and mutual respect will draw out greatness from their dogs and will be rewarded beyond their wildest expectations with a deep and lasting bond. Dogs are among the most honest creatures on earth. They are straight forward, uncomplicated and respond instinctively to the stimuli in their lives according to the principles of pack membership. Many years of experience have shown me that any behavioural problems dogs experience are usually caused by humans who misunderstand their dog's behaviour and psychology.

It isn't useful to attribute human qualities and human psychology to our dogs. They are simply wonderful in their own right and first, foremost and last biologically wired as dogs. They strive to please us because they are pack-driven, although we may like to attribute our human emotions to their actions. If they were wild dogs, living in a dog pack, with no human interaction, they would strive to please their pack leader in the same way they seek to please us, because it's the way they are wired in order to ensure their survival in the group as well as their pack's survival in its environment.

An example of smother-love made an impression on me when I supervised a busy boarding kennel many years ago. Earl was a lovely Pointer who routinely came into the kennels two or three times a year for a break from his artificial existence. He was a big, strong dog with a gentle nature. His life in a small apartment where he was dressed up in human clothes and fussed over was miles away from the purpose for which his breed was created; to run miles across country, flushing out birds and retrieving them from waterways.

Earl's mistress smothered him with love, but she was wise enough to recognise that when he broke out with eczema and chewed the end of his tail until it bled, his nerves were getting the better of him. A four week holiday in the kennels, where he was allowed to be a dog rather than a pampered child, cleared up the eczema and gave his mutilated tail a chance to heal while we treated it. When his liver coloured coat had grown back over the red raw patches, and the bloodied tip of his tail had hair growing back on it again, he would go home renewed in mind and body until we got the next telephone call from his owner again in two or three months.

There are some dog breeds which were developed specifically as lapdogs and these little ones are more suited to a fairy floss lifestyle. But most breeds were developed for specific functions, and the closer we can create an environment for our canine friends which suits their origins of purpose, the happier and more settled our dogs will be.

The Australian Cobberdog is born to serve, it's in his blood. Not as a slave to our whims and fancies, but for a higher purpose. He excels in the areas of therapy and assistance, and as a medical alert dog, or as a best friend for autistic children, but not every home has these specific needs. In the average family environment this remarkable dog's deepest longings are requited through training him to do simple things that give him a purpose in his own mind for being. He is capable of being aware of, and responding appropriately, to the slightest gestures from his family members in day to day life, even to his humans' facial expressions. To experience this precious bond with a dog is truly inspiring and quite unforgettable. Training your Australian Cobberdog is not merely an acceptable and sensible thing to do as it is with all dogs. It mimics his true calling, makes him whole and enables him to enrich your own life beyond your wildest dreams.

## INTRODUCING YOUR DOG AND YOUR NEW BABY

I'm often asked by young families how they should introduce their dog and their new baby. New babies are very demanding of parents' time and attention, and understandably, great dog owners can be concerned initially, that the dog, who is already a treasured family member, may feel left out and become jealous of the baby. I felt the same apprehension and concern when I was in the same position so I share my own experience because it turned out so spectacularly successful.

When my daughter was born, I had German Shepherd Dogs, and I wanted the introduction of my baby and the dogs to be a good one so that right from the start, they didn't feel their place threatened within the family. I didn't want them to resent the baby, thinking that she was taking my attention and love away from them, and although I strongly felt the nervousness of a new mother, I still didn't want my protection of the baby being translated by the dogs as shutting them out.

On the day I came home from the hospital, the dogs were very curious about the small bundle in my arms. I sat down with her in an armchair in the lounge room and the dogs crowded close, sniffing, tails wagging, but uncertain about what was going on. I asked them to sit and praised them quietly when they did. I started talking to them in a relaxed and loving way, explaining that this was our new family member and I chatted away, sharing with them the fun times we were all going to have together. Their eyes were fixed on the baby, but I didn't make any protective gestures towards her. It wasn't easy for a young mother! I didn't expect them to understand what I was saying, but I figured that the tone of my voice and the emotion behind what I was saying would create a particular energy around us. I used their favourite words a lot; the words I normally used when I told them how much I loved them.

While I was talking, I casually unwrapped the baby's feet from her bunny rugs and turned her around on my knees with her feet facing the dogs. My little daughter Angela was born with a deformed foot, and it was encased in a light support similar to a plaster cast, but softer, that seemed to fascinate them. Lolita was the first to notice it. She was a sable adult female who was recognized by the others as their leader. Whatever she decided about this strange new little creature would set the tone for the others. Her ears were pricked sharply and her muzzle was barely an inch from Angela's tiny feet and I trusted with all my heart that my dog savvy would be on the knocker.

When Lolita began to lick Angela's toes, ever so gently, I breathed a big sigh of relief.

They each had a turn at sniffing and licking at the baby's feet, then I stood up and carried her into her room where I put her in her crib while the dogs watched with great interest. Then I left the room, calling them with me and closed the door behind me. We trooped outside and I played with them, and gave them treats. I wanted them to know from the start that they were not being excluded, and I also wanted to give them time to think about what had just happened before they met bubs again.

It turned out so much better than I expected and hoped it would. I was careful over the coming days that I didn't send the dogs away when I was attending to the baby, and that their routine wasn't changed in favour of her. It was summer time when she was born, and on the days when I set the pram outside in the shade of the garden, it warmed my heart when I noticed that the dogs chose to lie down around her pram. It was as if they were guarding her. When she cried inside her room, they would run to her door and back to me, with a little yelp or bark, ,as if they were letting me know that she needed me. As she grew, they were her devoted companions and it was all a wonderful experience. I think the first meeting between dogs and baby was instrumental in settling the stage for the future. Perhaps that beautiful love transmitted from the dogs to her, may have been partly responsible for what was to be a lifelong love and commitment to dogs by my daughter.

# Breeding

I have sometimes wondered why I love to breed animals. Throughout my adult life I have bred Arabian horses, Quarter horses, stud goats and sheep, Angus cattle, Persian cats and several pure breeds of dog. Personally, I see nothing wrong with breeding for profit in return for the expenditure and long hours of hard work put in, but I discounted this as the motivating factor, since I tend to spend more on my animals than I could hope to get back in return. Breeding animals brings with it great responsibilities. When we breed, we are responsible for bringing new life into the world. Ethical dog breeding entails a lot of sleepless nights, countless cancelled leisure activities, the heartbreak of loss that can't be avoided if we breed often or long enough, and many disappointments along the way; some of them very costly in financial terms. So what is it I wondered, that makes a human being willing to sacrifice so much for the sake of breeding animals?

Perhaps this is a question that aspiring new dog breeders need to ask themselves, because once we understand our own motivation, we are then able to plot our course, and plan our breeding strategies with a purpose and a goal in mind. It never hurts to begin a long journey aided by a map!

I deeply appreciate the beauty of a well conformed, healthy animal or plant and I came to the conclusion that for me, breeding is about striving to improve the quality of the animals I am responsible for bringing into being and the immense satisfaction of producing a new generation better than the last. The joy of witnessing the miracle of new birth has not waned throughout the years, and the expectation of seeing the living, breathing results of my plans and aspirations, still brings me incredible pleasure and a sense of achievement and fulfilment.

People frequently ask me how I can bear to part with my puppies when it's time for them to leave for their forever homes. I admit that I do shed a few tears sometimes, but I see myself as a foster mother. While the youngsters are with me I pour my heart and soul into them, but this is to prepare them for their future lives, and when my work is done and it's time for them to go out into the world, the joy they bring into the lives of others enriches my own life in a meaningful way.

## THE PLAN

When people begin their breeding adventure with a breed that someone else has already developed hundreds of years ago, the choices of where to start are not difficult because a type has already been set and it isn't as easy to make mistakes that will drastically alter the outcome of the breed. However when we are working with a new breed in development, the implications of our choices can affect the overall future of the breed in ways that may not be able to be reversed.

We probably have decided how many dogs we want to keep, and what sizes and coat type we would like to have, before we plunge ahead, but there are still traps for the unwary. Experienced breeders are well aware that producing quality is not as simple as breeding the best to the best. If it were, everyone could breed perfect dogs. In reality, some bloodlines 'nick' (blend well) with certain others and different ones don't. When we look at dogs we see their phenotype (what is able to be seen) but we are working with genotype (the genetic material that is made up of a complex mix of multiple genes in the ancestors) and there is no accurate guarantee which way these genes are going to interact together.

The more we study pedigrees, and delve into past outcomes of particular combinations, the easier it will be to make wise choices when selecting breeding partners. Even then, nothing is certain, and I classify the expected results into three categories; the possible, the probable and the impossible. Nothing is certain! But this is part of the fascination of breeding.

The study of genetics is a mammoth undertaking, and to discuss it fully is not within the scope of this handbook, but it is relatively simple to plan a breeding program for preferred colours due to the DNA colour tests which are now available. Over the past few years I have observed the worrying trend of an obsessive focus on colour. There was a time when families impressed on their breeder, their need for a particular kind of nature in their new puppy. It was all about temperament, intuition, and perhaps gender and size. I think the wide range of colours in the Australian Cobberdog is what has led to people becoming obsessed with a particular colour, often at the expense of the more important qualities of the dog. This is a great pity, because it engenders a need in breeders, to focus on breeding for the most popular colours, rather than concentrating on other important aspects of the dogs they are breeding. I once returned someone's puppy deposit and refused to sell them a puppy, because the lady of the house only wanted a dog which would match the décor of her home. I wondered what would happen to her dog if she decided to redecorate!

I think that it is important for breeders to communicate openly with one another, and to share what is happening within the breed, including health problems which unavoidably raise their heads from time to time. Unfortunately many breeders take a personal stance on this and can tend to hide the faults which crop up in their dogs, due to feeling that this in some way reflects negatively on their breeding programs. Others can become 'kennel blind' which means that they can see no wrong with their own dogs, but invariably point their fingers at dogs belonging to others. The reality is that no matter how meticulously careful and conscientious a breeder may be, none can with honesty guarantee that they will never breed a dog with a genetic or hereditary health problem. The complexity of genetic inheritance and the influence of environmental conditions outside the breeder's control, combine to simply make it impossible, so it is no reflection on a breeder if despite their best efforts they do breed an occasional defective dog. In an ideal world, breeders will regard each other as brothers and sisters who all have the same objectives in mind; the future of the breed they all love.

## CHOOSING BREEDING DOGS AND PUPPIES

A very nice puppy from a litter of good even type across the litter, is a better choice for breeding than an outstanding individual from an otherwise ordinary litter. The reason for this, is that the above-average phonetic traits (those you can see) in the outstanding puppy, have only expressed themselves in one individual from the litter, whereas the very nice puppy shares his traits with his siblings, which indicates that his genetic influence should be more stable. Not every puppy left entire is a suitable breeding dog just because it is the best in its litter. The Breed Standard paints a picture of the ideal, and each puppy should be measured against this ideal which should be adhered to as closely as possible if a breeder is to make progress. Coat type and other traits can be worked on, but structural soundness is an absolute must as a foundation for the building blocks on which a breed is established, when considering a puppy to be kept or sold for breeding.

Soundness demonstrates itself best at the trot which is a two-time diagonal gait which reveals any lameness or weakness in anatomy. This is the reason that all show dogs, including galloping breeds, are trotted out for the judges. In quadrupeds, impulsion starts from the rear end, and a hind foot takes the first step; transferring its power forward through loins, hips and back to the shoulders which in turn, transmit it through a forward step. Even if angulation of the stifle and short strong hocks are adequate enough to generate a powerful and deep step from the rear, motion will be blocked if the shoulders are too straight and upright to allow full extension of the front leg. This would result in a shorter stride in front than from behind and synchronicity is lost. A good judge will notice the up and down movement in the poorly balanced dog's top line (back) and a jerky step rather than the flowing gait and level top line of the correctly balanced individual.

In the following photographs, the picture on the left shows an adult bitch at full extension of her trot because her front paw has just touched the ground. She appears to have good reach and drive from behind, but because of her upright shoulder, she is stepping shorter in front, and landing heavily on her forehand (note her loins which are higher than her withers). Overall, she is a nice type of bitch, but her lack of balanced conformation could lead to unsoundness with OCDs in later life, such as Hip or Elbow Dysplasia or arthritis caused by stresses to her joints, ligaments and tendons. Her action will be jerky and lacking in fluidity. This dog will prefer to gallop, rather than trot, and may pace (trot with same-side front and back limbs stepping together instead of diagonally) especially when moving off slowly. Compare her photo to the one on the right, which shows a correctly conformed adult female. Her loins are rounded to absorb the transfer of movement and her shoulder has freely transferred power from rear to front allowing for a powerful long reach.

The sixteen weeks old puppy in the next photo, is not quite at full extension of his trot as his front paw hasn't yet touched the ground. Yet because the angle of his shoulder blade is symmetrical to that of his stifle, he is already balanced, which allows him a long elastic stride which places minimal stress on his joints His short hocks give him the strength for the push off stride, and long well angulated stifles enable him to reach so far beneath himself that even at such a young age, his loins have rounded as a natural shock absorber. The symmetrical balance of his shoulder allows his powerful movement to be transmitted through to his front end, permitting unrestricted length of stride with his front legs. His top line will remain level when he trots and there will be no jerky movement or pacing.

*Correct movement at full extension-5months old puppy*

Correct skeletal structure denotes what is called 'form to function' which means that the dog's conformation (build) allows natural movement with the least possible stress on the dog's body. This is one reason that the Australian Cobberdog Breed Standard insists that there be no exaggerations. If breeders focus on producing dogs with for example, an exaggeratedly curved stifle, on the premise that if well angulated is good, then more is better, this results in unbalanced conformation and the lack of soundness that goes along with it. Many dogs may look beautiful when they are standing still, but it is in movement that the flaws in their conformation are revealed.

One example of tragic outcomes from exaggeration is the German Shepherd Dog. I was still breeding them when the 40 year import ban was lifted on the breed being imported into Australia, and there was a rush of local breeders eager to improve on the straight stifles of the inbred Australian dogs. Many of the dogs bred during this new era had such steeply angled hindquarters, that they looked as if they were half sitting down when they were standing and unfortunately so many breeders bred for this exaggeration that it affected the German Shepherd Dog breed permanently.

This condition was so serious that Dr Trevor Turner[20] noted in his article "Anal Furunculosis' that it was considered that with the increasing angulation seen in the breed, the close lying tail prevented air circulation around the perineal area, and in consequence allowed the infection to spread.

---

20 Ref: Trevor Turner BVetMed, MRCVS, FRSH, MCIAb, MAE -Anal Furunculosis 15th June 2003 h ttp://www.videxgsd.com/Anal_Furunculosis_TT2.htm

*Green Gables Sir Luciano of CHBK, an excellent example of a well-proportioned dog. (Photo courtesy of Green Gables Labradoodles USA)*

When we are breeding to improve a particular feature in our dogs, we should remember that like produces like. Let's suppose that we have a female who has a narrow head, and because we want to improve the heads on the puppies, we mate her with a male whose head is too broad. We could assume that the genes for narrow heads and those for overly broad heads might combine and we could be lucky enough to get the heads we are after across the litter. In reality what we will get, is some puppies with narrow heads, and others with overly broad heads, not something in between. We need to appreciate that it takes time to work through an improvement program, and that we are unlikely to see progress in too many traits all at the one time. This is a good argument for beginning a breeding program with dogs which come as close to the Breed Standard as possible. A top breeding puppy or adult will cost more, but in the long run will save years of trial and error, which all equate to many times as much as the initial outlay for obtaining great breeding stock in the first place.

## MATING THE DOG AND BITCH

Australian Cobberdog female puppy will come into her first season (her first heat) any time from six months of age to twelve months or even older. When she should be mated will vary according to her physical and emotional maturity as well as her bodily condition. Some bitches are still puppies themselves at a year to eighteen months old while others may be already mature. Males can be sexually active as young as six or seven months of age. But they are still babies, and seldom emotionally mature Your enough to be allowed to mate. If a male of this age is given a bitch, he can be so overwhelmed by the experience that he may even refuse to mate again for many months while he tries to work out what happened. This is called over facing a young stud. It is far better to wait until he is at least twelve months old before presenting him with his first bitch. He should be given an experienced female for his initial mating. She will patiently put up with his clumsy attempts to work out which end is which, and may even try to help him, which will give him the confidence to keep trying. A young or flighty bitch may snap at him and frighten him off, which may damage his self-esteem, and make him a reluctant or nervous stud for the future.

An entire male dog may give us our first indication that our female is thinking about coming into season. He may pay special attention to nuzzling behind her ears, where glands secrete an odour that he recognises but which our own senses are not acute enough to smell. When this happens, we can usually count on our girl coming into heat in about three weeks. For those who don't have an entire male on hand, our first indicator of the onset of season will be a swelling of the female's vulva, so it pays to be familiar with its normal size and shape. Not every female bleeds early, and some do not bleed at all, so don't rely on seeing spotting unless you know your bitch's tendencies.

If she does bleed, the first flow should be a bright dark red in colour. If it is a rusty brown, or has a greenish tinge, take her to your vet immediately for a vaginal swab in case she has an infection. If picked up early, most infections will respond to a broad spectrum antibiotic and she can still be mated during that season.

As her heat progresses, the colour of her discharge will pale day by day until it is a pinkish straw coloured issue, of slightly thicker consistency than before. When the colour has all but disappeared, the crown of her vulva will have softened and will be spongy and prominent. When you stroke her hind end with your hand, she will fling her tail to one side (called 'flagging') and her vulva will 'wink'. She is now ready to accept a male. This usually occurs between day eleven and day fourteen of her cycle, but can vary from one bitch to another.

If you intend to mate her using Artificial Insemination, (A.I.) she should be taken to your vet from about day five or six, to commence a series of blood tests and cytology, to determine the optimum time for insemination.

Natural matings are best done either in the early morning or in the later afternoon to early evening, and neither dog nor bitch should have been fed for at least four hours beforehand. Many stud dogs appreciate a bowl of fresh water being handy in the honeymoon suite and a few laps help to rejuvenate them from all the huffing and puffing going on. Some breeders like both dogs to be on leash both before and during mating, but I think it is more natural and much nicer for them to be allowed to flirt and play together until things start to look serious. When the bitch stands willingly for the dog to mount her, with her tail to the side, I then pop her onto a leash long enough to give her freedom, but short enough that I can reach her quickly if she needs assistance. I like to leave the male dog off leash, because they have their own individual rituals and will often prefer to mount from a favourite side, or may be shy if someone stands too close by.

*The bitch is relaxed and willing on a loose leash,*
*with watchful attendants nearby*

Sometimes a bitch can get so excited and exhilarated with what's happening especially once the dog is tied (joined) inside of her, that she may fling herself onto the ground and roll. This is potentially dangerous for the male, because if he is not experienced, his penis could be broken. It is comforting to the female and easier on the stud, if you hold both dogs' tails in one hand, close to their rumps during the tie. This can take anything from several minutes up to an hour, so I find it helpful to have a chair handy! If the stud dog ejaculates inside the female but without tying, this is called a slip mating. It is possible for a bitch to get pregnant from a slip mating, but it is much better if there is a tie, even for a few minutes. If only a slip mating has occurred, the stud dog's owner should give you an extension of time to pay the stud fee, until an ultra sound confirming pregnancy is done, four weeks after the mating.

*Holding the tails close to their rumps*

Canine Artificial Insemination (A.I.) using frozen semen has become popular in recent years. This is probably due to two factors; geographic distances between the owner of a stud dog and the bitch's owner and some stud dog owners being reluctant to put their dogs at risk of injury or disease. When a stud dog is particularly valuable he may be collected and frozen as insurance in case something happens to him, or so that his direct influence on his breed can continue after his death. A.I. can be expensive, because once the stud fee is paid, veterinary costs must also be met. The rate of success depends largely on the post-thawing quality of the semen, the technician's experience and expertise, and the availability of the bitch when her cytology and blood tests indicate the optimal time for mating. Post thawing motility of the semen should be 60% or better for the best results.

When the semen has been purchased it can be sent through the post to the reproductive veterinary facility where the A.I. is to be carried out. When semen is collected from the dog, an extender will have been added such as egg yolk. This protects the fragile spermatozoa while in storage or traveling.

During transit it travels in a special temperature controlled container and is stored at the clinic until it is needed. Some vets charge for this and others provide it as a complimentary service.

Semen can be frozen either as 'straws' or 'pellets'. Reproductive Veterinarians have their own preferred methods for insemination which can be either directly into the cervix via the vagina, with the bitch's owner standing by her side, or by surgery under anaesthetic, which requires an overnight stay at the clinic. I think the former is by far the best method for the bitch's sake, but not all veterinarians will do it this way. A.I. can also be performed with fresh semen. This necessitates the stud dog being collected at the vet clinic with the bitch also in attendance, and the semen inserted via the vagina immediately after collection and appraisal for quality. A maiden stud dog, or one who hasn't mated for a long time, will have non fertile ejaculate in his first collection and may require a second one to be done a day or two later, so this should be taken into consideration when working out timing for the bitch.

*Using on on-heat bitch to collect for insemination or freezing of the semen. She is being allowed to sit because she is not the intended recipient of this dog's semen*

*Ejaculate being collected into a specimen cup*

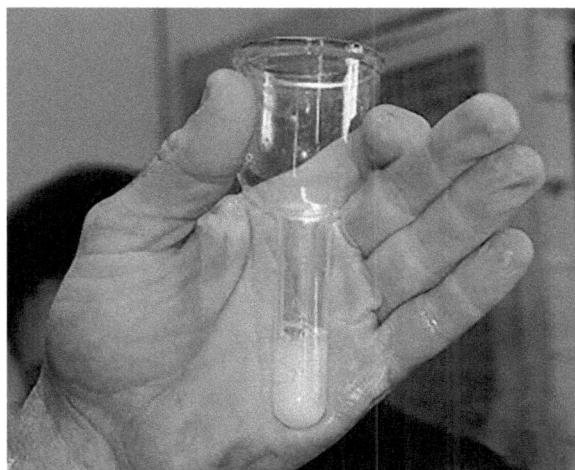

*A good quality collection before extender is added*

Gestation is 61 to 63 days, although artificially inseminated females often deliver their puppies a day or so early. After a natural mating, there can be a variation of the whelping date of up to four days on either side without undue problems. But if dog and bitch are allowed to run together for the duration of her heat, it may be impossible to estimate the time of fertilisation, and this could present problems if she goes overdue because it will be difficult to calculate whether or not a caesarean is needed. When the female is flagging her tail to the side in response to gentle stroking of her inner thighs, she should be ready for mating, and when two good ties have been observed over three days the two should be separated.

Entire male dogs can smell an in-season female from miles away, and they will go to incredible lengths to get at her if we are not very careful. I have known males to chew holes in a strong wire mesh fence, and solid wooden fences; to dig holes under gates, and to scale amazing heights to get to a bitch on heat. A bitch will allow other males to mate her even after she has already been bred and is pregnant. This habit has been responsible for many a surprise package when the litter is born!

If our female is overweight, it is necessary to put her on a veterinary-approved reducing diet well before the expected time of her mating. Conception rates are better for females on a rising plane of nutrition but not already fat. It's as if nature tells them that good times are ahead, so it's okay to bring pups into the world. The reverse can apply if she is getting less food. Imminent pregnancy is never a good time to attempt weight loss.

## FAILED PREGNANCIES AND THE 'FADING PUPPY SYNDROME'

From my experience it is safe to say that most problems with bitches who fail to fall pregnant to natural matings and stud dogs with poor fertility are usually caused by bacterial infections, as can be irregularly occurring heat cycles. If your female has missed seasons or pregnancies for no apparent reason, your vet should do a vaginal swab for laboratory testing as soon as she comes into season the next time, because there may be no outward signs of an underlying infection. In the case of a stud dog with poor fertility, a throat and sheath swab should be taken for testing, as an infected dog can pass on his infection to a healthy bitch during mating. The 'fading puppy syndrome', in which newborn puppies fail to thrive and die for no apparent reason within days of birth, can also be traced to their mother's bacterial infection, which is transmitted to the puppies during their trip along the birth canal The normal healthy vagina of a bitch has a series of bacteria, including streptococci, (including Betga-haemolytic streptococci), staphylococci, Escherichia coli (E Coli) and more, with each one being controlled by the others in order to sustain a regulated balance. The problems arise when one bacterium becomes more prominent, and this causes an imbalance regardless of how slight the predominance of a single bacterium may be.

Your vet may prescribe courses of a drug such as Synulox, at selected intervals once a suspect bitch manages to become pregnant, to prevent contamination of foetal fluids and bacterial contamination of the female's milk, which in turn can cause mastitis, usually resulting from a streptococci infection.

Some scholars suggest that the pheromone related 'Bruce effect' [21] or pregnancy block, first noted in 1959 by Hilda M Bruce, and which refers to the tendency for female rodents to terminate their pregnancies when exposed to the scent of an unfamiliar male, may also occur in canines. More recent scientific research confirms the Bruce effect does occur in several species other than rodents. It may be worth considering in the case of a bitch which has failed to conceive or maintain her pregnancy for no apparent reason, and if the Bruce effect is a possibility then the bitch should not be allowed within scent range of any canine entire male other than the one she was mated with, for the duration of her pregnancy.

---

[22] Ref: Bruce, Hilda M. (1959). "An Exteroceptive Block to Pregnancy in the Mouse". *Nature* 184 (4680): 105. doi: 10.1038/184105a0. PMID 13805128,Ref: A Bruce Effect in Wild Geladas,Science, 9 March 2012:Vol. 335 no. 6073 pp. 1222-1225, DOI: 10.1126/science.1213600

## THE IN-WHELP BITCH

Early signs that our female has taken to her mating, may be either in-
creased appetite or conversely a loss of appetite for the first three weeks,
sometimes accompanied by 'morning sickness' and she may be more emotionally needy and clingy than usual. Her nipples may be more prominent
and turn a darker brighter pink for a few days three weeks post mating.
Some vets and breeders are able to palpate the bitch and feel the tiny babies
slip through their fingers like a string of pearls, although I have never been
any good at this. In any event, if we want to be sure, we can take our female
to the vet for an ultra sound at around four weeks after mating. She could
be scanned sooner than this, but I like to leave it until four weeks because
the skeletal structure of the puppies is already formed, which means that
she is less likely to re-absorb her foetuses. Some females show no physical
signs of their pregnancy until six weeks along, when they may suddenly
'pop' almost overnight. These ones can really keep you guessing if an ultra
sound hasn't been done.

It is important to avoid stress to a bitch for twenty one days following an
artificial insemination. During this time she should not indulge in rough
play with other dogs, nor should she be allowed to jump up onto, nor down
from high places during this critical period.

For the first four to five weeks a healthy well-conditioned pregnant
female doesn't need any changes to her normal nutritious diet, but as the
pregnancy progresses past six weeks, she will do better on several small
meals each day, as she may not be able to ingest the quantity of food she
needs at one or two sittings due to the pressure of a full uterus reducing
the capacity of her stomach.

We may feel tempted to supplement our expectant mother with Calcium
but studies show that this is contraindicated. As long she is on a quality

THE COMPLETE AUSTRALIAN COBBERDOG          109

diet, supplementation is not only unnecessary, but it can suppress her natural Parathyroid releasing hormone so that when she really needs extra calcium while nursing her puppies, she won't have the hormone balance to get it. This can create a very dangerous situation, setting up the bitch for eclampsia, which may be avoided by not supplementing with calcium. [23]

Pregnant females may safely have an occasional mucus discharge either clear or pink tinged, but if the discharge is a darker colour, or contains blood or pus, seek veterinary help immediately.

Set up her whelping box in a cosy quiet place away from draughts and heavy foot traffic, and introduce her to it a good week before she is due to give birth so that she feels comfortable in it and in its location. Some breeders like to have a rail around the inside perimeter so that the puppies can move under it if their mother accidentally lies on them. Newspaper provides good insulation for the floor of the box, with washable rugs or blankets on top.

## ONSET OF LABOUR

Some bitches give no indication that they are about to go into labour. I once had a female many years ago who first taught me this. Rutlands Angel was used to sleeping on my bed and because I wasn't expecting her to give birth for another few days, I hadn't yet transferred her to the whelping box. She lay beside me with her head on the other pillow and I was looking into her face, close to mine, telling her how beautiful she was, when I noticed her eyes change to a distant expression. A slight ripple ran through her body, and to my amazement, out slid a puppy onto my bed covers. After a quick transition into the whelping box, she had eight more babies in the same effortless fashion.

When the bitch's whelping date is near, it will help to organize your schedule around the big event. A few hours before whelping, the temperature of most females will drop slightly, which should give you about twelve hours' notice and enable you to arrange things so that you are on hand when she goes into labour. The normal temperature for an adult dog is between 100 and 105.2 degrees Fahrenheit, and with this variance in the normal range, it will help if you are familiar with her usual temperature. It is helpful to take your female's temperature several times daily a week before she is due, so that you are familiar with her pattern of temperature, remembering that if she is excited from playing with the kids, or greeting visitors her temperature will be elevated until she has settled down again.

Thankfully, most expectant mothers will give you advance notice that labour is imminent. The first stage may last anything from two to twelve hours with regular uterine contractions. She may scratch up and chew chew her bedding, appear nervous and unsettled, and pant, shiver and tremble. Some may vomit or have diarrhoea, and food or water is usually refused.

When her cervix is fully dilated, the second stage of labour commences, with more powerful contractions, and less time in between. Puppies usually present either face or hind feet first. When it is a hind end presentation, the birth of that puppy can take longer, and your gentle assistance may be appreciated by holding its hind legs and helping it out with a gentle downwards pull towards her hocks. Time this with the mother's contractions, otherwise you may damage her or her whelp.

It is normal for the in-labour female to take lengthy rests of up to an hour or more in between delivering a single puppy, or after having two or three in quick succession. But if she is having strong contractions with no result for longer than an hour a call to the vet is in order. Some experienced breeders use a prescription hormone drug called Oxytocin and inject a slow whelping or tired bitch either intramuscularly or subcutaneously to stimulate uterine contractions. I wouldn't advise novice breeders to use this approach, because if a puppy is stuck, and the Oxytocin starts powerful contractions, the bitch's uterus could rupture which would kill her. As well as this, Oxytocin may cause premature detachment of the unborn puppy which would result in stillbirth. Puppies stimulate natural oxytocin release in the mother by nursing, but if the puppies are slow to drink, or born tired from a difficult labour the mother may not have produced enough. When a normal whelping is finished, and the mother is resting contentedly, an Oxytocin shot will expel any retained afterbirths, flush her out and close her uterus, which helps to avoid possible infection.

Presentation can be either head first, or breech, both are normal in the bitch. Breech puppies though, do need to be delivered are quickly once they are in the pelvic canal. You'll know this by their hind end hanging out of the mother's vulva. I find it helpful in these instances to 'feather' (massage) the roof of her vagina with my gloved fingers and be ready to hook them behind the head or the hips.

## WHEN TO CONSIDER A C SECTION

A bitch who has not produced a puppy in three hours of serious contractions, is a c-section candidate. It makes no sense to wait until you have an exhausted bitch with stressed puppies from hard labour. I would rather opt for a c-section on an unstressed bitch unnecessarily, than take the risk of being forced to do one on a stressed and exhausted female.

If an ultra sound has shown that the bitch is having only one puppy you should consult your vet about the advisability of doing an elective c-section, because a single puppy is often much larger, and more difficult if not impossible, for the female to deliver by herself. It is the puppies who stimulate labour and in a normal sized litter, the pressure coming from further up the line helps to keep the puppies moving. Conversely, when the litter is very large, it may be kinder to consider an elective c-section rather than allow the bitch to struggle through many hours of hard labour, only to have to face surgery anyway, when she is already stressed and tired. The latter should not usually be of concern with the Australian Cobberdog though, at least not in the short term, because as I developed the breed, I selectively bred for easy birthing as one of its health attributes. However as time goes on, other breeders may not continue with this selective process and over generations of retaining poor whelpers as breeding stock, the breed could lose its current benefit of easy labour and the joy of effortless delivery of the puppies.

A large sire over a smaller bitch is not an indication for a c-section. Birth size is primarily determined by the bitch herself in a normal sized litter. The most common causes of dystocia (difficulties in labour) are mal-presentations and uterine inertia and these have nothing to do with the size of the bitch and sire.

Puppies are born encased in a sack which can be surprisingly tough, or it may break easily, releasing the protective fluid which will come in a rush and wet the bedding and the mother's hind legs. I find it helpful to place a wad of newspaper or absorbent paper directly beneath her rear end when a birth is imminent. This can then be discarded into the rubbish bag, to keep the nest as dry and clean as possible in between births. If your bitch is the kind who becomes so absorbed in every new birth that she isn't careful to avoid hurting the whelps already born, you could place most of them into a separate box, within her sight, warmed with a heating pad or hot water bottle, and covered with a soft towel or blanket, until the newest puppy is safely born and the mother has regained her composure. Some bitches appreciate this and others worry about the puppies being removed from the nest, so you will need to use your own discretion depending on how your female reacts when you transfer the first puppy into the basket.

Maiden bitches (first time mothers) will sometimes fail to break open the birth sack of the first puppy, so you should be ready to help her or you may lose the puppy through suffocation or drowning in the fluid. Once the placentas detach and delivery is under way, there is no exchange of oxygen from the mother to the unborn, and when the air supply in the birth sack is used up, the puppy will suffocate if the sack is not broken in time to expose the puppy's nose to the air. Hind end presentations will usually need the puppy's nostrils to be cleared of mucus and fluid, using a soft absorbent paper towel. Discard the towel after use and take a fresh one for the next puppy. If the baby is slow to breathe, or seems lethargic, rub it briskly with the towel. If it squeaks all the better because this will help the mother's maternal instincts to kick in and she will take over and start to lick him. Give her the opportunity to chew through the cord herself before you decide to cut it for her. If it is necessary for you to do it, use sterilised blunt scissors so as to make a rough cut which won't bleed, or use umbilical cord scissors especially made for the purpose. Be careful not to pull against the navel as you sever the cord. Rough handling of this area could result in an umbilical hernia which will need to be surgically repaired a little later on.

Some breeders will take away the afterbirths from the mother, but I let mine eat them as nature intended. They are a rich source of nutrition and they stimulate milk production in the bitch. I believe that the benefits to the bitch outweigh the inconvenience of the cleansing bout of diarrhoea that sometimes follows.

When the weather is hot, she will appreciate some ice cubes to lick during her resting periods, and a small drink of water to refresh her mouth. If the labour has been a long one and she seems to be tired, I will offer her a small drink of warm lactose-free milk, with an egg yolk and a teaspoonful of honey or glucose mixed through. This is usually gratefully accepted.

When the bitch has settled down and is finished having her litter, it is a good time to clean out most of the soiled bedding and dispose of it while she is busy with her new brood. For maiden bitches, I leave just a small amount in one corner, because the scent of it will help her to feel confident of her nest so that she doesn't try to carry her newborns out of the whelping box and take them to another place.

Heat lamps overhead, or a heated pad in the whelping box are generally used to make sure the puppies are kept warm, but be careful that there is an area in the box that is free of a heating device so that the bitch can move away from it if she gets too hot. Newborn puppies although blind and deaf, have acute senses which draw them towards warmth. If they are too content lying on a heated pad, they may not seek out their mother often enough to drink, and she may also leave the box for too long a period if she feels uncomfortably hot. This could dehydrate the puppies.

Newborn puppies should gain weight each day, so it is helpful to weigh them daily and keep a record of their weight so that you can take immediate steps to correct anything that is stalling their growth and development. If a puppy is not progressing, and you are concerned about a possible infection take the puppy's temperature by gently inserting a digital thermometer into its rectum. The normal rectal temperature of a newborn puppy is between 96 and 100 degrees Fahrenheit

## TROUBLE SHOOTING

Occasionally you may get a bleeder puppy, if the bitch has chewed the cord too close to the baby's stomach and if this happens, it is critical that you stop the bleeding as quickly as possible. There are several different ways you could do this. I like to tie it off with fine cotton, making sure that there are no long trailing ends for the mother to catch in her teeth. There are bleeder swabs and tips available in whelping kits and can be purchased on the internet. A handy emergency tip if you are caught unprepared is to hold a little piece of doubled newspaper against the raw edge for a few minutes or hold an ice cube against the bleed.

If you need to separate a very young puppy from his mother for some reason, or are bottle feeding or tube feeding an orphan, you will need to stroke his bottom and penis and in the case of a female, her bottom and vagina, with a soft tissue or swab, at each feed and a few times in between, to stimulate elimination. They are unable to pass poo or urine by themselves, and their mother does this for them when they are with her.

If a puppy has had a long or difficult birth, it might show little signs of life and lie there without appearing to breathe. Waste no time and quickly wipe its throat and nostrils out with a clean dry swab, then cradle the infant firmly, face down, in both of your hands. Support its head between your fingers on each side and shake the puppy firmly downwards four or five times. This will push his lungs against his ribcage and help to expel any mucus or fluid, which should be wiped away again. Massage firmly with your fingers, from chest to throat, and rough it up a little to get it to squeak.

Each newborn in the litter must get its mother's colostrum preferably within 12 hours, or at most, within 24 hours. After this, it won't be absorbed and maternal immunity will be lost. The colostrum must be the first thing to enter the stomach. Bitches that are recovering from a caesarian section (may be unable to feed the puppies yet) or that are initially reluctant to feed the pups for other reasons can be milked of their colostrum and this can be fed to them with a bottle or by stomach tubing. If the bitch has no colostrum, or leaks her colostrum early, the veterinarian can take plasma from the bitch and give it to the puppies either orally in milk formula, (within the first 12-24 hours), or via plasma transfusion (if over 24 hours).

Puppies can tend to have favourite nipples, even as newborns. If there are more nipples than puppies, one or more may not be nursed on and could very quickly become hard and hot with mastitis. Once the puppies have decided on their favourite nipples, and left others not nursed on, some udders may build up with milk. This is a precursor to painful mastitis. If you feel an udder that is bursting full, squeeze a little bit of milk out to make sure it is not clotting, and if not, try to encourage some of the puppies to nurse on it. If you are not successful, then it will be necessary to express some of the milk several times a day to relieve the pressure. If when you do this, the milk coming from that nipple is thick, or similar to scrambled eggs, then mastitis is already setting in and the vet should be called without delay.

If you're having trouble getting a puppy onto a nipple, try another one instead, and don't assume that a puppy is drinking because you can see it sucking. Some puppies will miss the nipple and suck on a piece of their mother's skin or fur, and just quietly fade away. Place your finger under each puppy's throat to feel if it is swallowing, especially during the first twenty four to forty eight hours. When baby puppies are getting enough to drink, their stomachs should look bulging, and disproportionately large to the rest of their body. If their sides are flat, they are not getting enough and may need to be supplemented especially if the mother is slow in letting down her milk. A good sign that shows a puppy is drinking is when you see its front paws treading and tiny tail quivering. I like to think of this as its very first tail wag!

Puppies are not able to regulate their own body temperature until they are nearly three weeks old, and there could be times when you find a very young puppy lying cold and stiff to the side of the whelping box because he has been separated from the warmth in the nest. His mouth may be gaping open and you might think that he is dead, but he could be suffering from hypothermia and quick action could save his life. I tuck a puppy like this beneath my clothing under my armpit while I run hot water into the sink and put a towel into the microwave or clothes dryer. When the water reaches a comfortable temperature for your own elbow, swish the puppy gently around in it while you softly massage his body and legs, taking care to keep his mouth clear of the water. Be careful not to let the water get cold. If you feel him begin to stir, and to make little movements on his own, you have saved him. Wrap him up in the warm towel and continue with the massage until he wriggles and squeaks. It is critical that you never try to feed a cold puppy or get him to nurse on his mother when he is cold, because this will certainly kill him.

## TAKING CARE OF THE NEW MOTHER

Your new mother may be reluctant to leave her newborns for the first couple of days, to go potty, so she should be put on the leash and taken outside at least for a few moments, several times daily until she is ready to come out of her own accord. The brief exercise will be good for her and will also help fluids to drain away which could cause infection if left stagnating inside. It is normal for her to have a discharge which may be pink in colour, clear, or a greenish black for a week after birthing. But if it is bright red, black and tarry, evil smelling, or looks like pus immediate vet attention will be necessary.

Thoroughly examine the bitch's udders and nipples every day. I once didn't know why the puppies were leaving one udder alone until I found that a single strand of their mother's coat had wrapped itself tightly around the nipple. This could have had serious consequences if it hadn't been discovered quickly. Hopefully, your new mother will be eating well and she should be allowed to have as much as she wants. If she has gone off her food, it is worth spoiling her and giving in to her whims until her appetite returns. Water should be refreshed several times a day. Water makes milk and if her face is a little dirty from changing her babies' nappies, she won't want to drink from the bowl if she has put her soiled mouth into it already.

## PREVENTING INFECTIOUS DISEASE

The puppies will have a measure of protection against infectious disease from the antibodies in their mother's colostrum, if she is current on her own vaccinations, or if she has been titre tested for appropriate vaccine levels in her blood, but they are still vulnerable until two weeks following completion of their own vaccination schedule. When puppies are still nursing on their mother at the time of vaccination, the antibodies in her milk can 'fight' with the vaccine, and some of the puppies in the litter can be unprotected despite the fact that they have been vaccinated.

Deadly killers such as Parvo Virus are the dread of every breeder, for despite their best efforts it is so easy for Parvo to enter the premises, either on someone's shoes, clothing, or on the tyres of cars. For this reason it is a good idea for a bitch and her puppies to be housed in an area where there is the least foot traffic from outside of the property. Your own family members could have unwittingly walked on an area while out shopping or coming home from school, where an infectious dog has been. Parvo will live for years in soil, grass and even concrete, and on surfaces which are regularly cleaned and the only disinfectant that can kill it is either bleach or the parvo-specific products now on the market. It isn't practical to spray every inch of your home on a daily basis, so shoes worn outside of your property should be changed once you get home, while puppies are in the home or yard.

One of the greatest dangers comes from well-meaning people who want to come and see your puppies. They may have visited other breeders on the way, or they may have unknowingly been in contact with an infectious dog or on the ground where one has been. When I was breeding Rough Coated Scotch Collies, my mentor was a wonderful woman and renowned breeder called Zora Mitchell of the famous Braeden Collie Kennels in Melbourne. Zora taught me the ropes about protecting puppies by insisting that visitors rub their shoes on bleach soaked mats, allow their hands to be sprayed with bleach, and wear a clean cotton shirt which she provided, over their clothes, before she allowed them near her dogs or puppies.

One Sunday afternoon a very nice family arrived at Zora's home to pick up the puppy they had ordered. They asked if they could see the siblings as well, so after the disinfecting process parents and children were permitted to play with the puppies and handle the adult dogs. Just as they were leaving, with their precious new puppy in the mother's arms, she turned to Zora and said that no one could imagine what this meant to her and her family, because their last puppy had died of Parvo six months ago. A distressed Zora gave them back their money and with-held the puppy until he would be older and less at risk. But it was too late. The puppy along with several of his siblings got Parvo and died while in the veterinary hospital getting treatment. That fateful visit resulted in Zora's property becoming endemic for Parvo and for years afterwards, raising each litter of puppies was a stressful and worrying time for Zora.

Breeders who are aware of the latent dangers, are faced with the choice of either keeping their puppies on the mother as well as feeding solid foods, and putting off the vaccinations until the puppies are seven or eight weeks old, or finishing the weaning process earlier and vaccinating earlier. Neither way is ideal, but the ever present threat of Parvo is too serious to be taken lightly.

## WEANING THE PUPPIES

I like to introduce solid food to my puppies when they are almost four weeks of age and the first thing I give them is natural, non flavoured, non sweetened yogurt. I figure that because they will soon be presented with meat and other foods for the first time, the yogurt settles their tummies and helps to keep the natural balance of the flora in their digestive systems. They seem to be instinctively aware of how good it is for them, because they dive straight into the bowl and lap like little champions. Some bitches are such good mothers that they keep their puppies so well stuffed with milk that the puppies can be difficult to persuade to eat solids, but I've never had puppies refuse the yogurt. I continue with the yogurt daily even when I have added shredded raw meat, with Dr Bruce's All Natural Complete Puppy Mix, eggs, cheese, lactose free milk and raw chicken necks to their diet. They have four meals daily to the age of seven weeks along with full access to their mother, until they are eight weeks old, when I begin to take their mother away for most of the day, and put her back with them for the night. When she is not with them I leave a good quality holistic kibble with them to nibble on in between their meal times, which by this time, have been cut back to three times daily. Although I am not an advocate for kibble, I realise that some of my puppies will go to families who will feed kibble, so it is important that their little systems recognise the stuff as 'food'.

Puppies need to learn social behaviour from their mother and she has much to teach them whilst they are still with her, so provided she is in excellent health herself and in top bodily condition, I leave the puppies with her until they are eight weeks old. When she has had enough of them drinking from her she lets them know in no uncertain terms but by then they are fully established on their solids. Some bitches will let you know that it's time to wean their puppies, by vomiting up their own partly digested meal in the bed with the puppies, but not all females will do this. During weaning, it is very important to inspect the bitch's udders daily, and feel them with your hands, to ensure that there is no build up of milk. As less is required of her, her own system will gradually decrease the amount produced.

Breeding one lovely dog to another lovely dog and hoping for lovely progeny is a random practice which has no structure and which will not produce consistent results. Dogs bred in this way will reflect the lack of planning that has gone into producing them and over time the breed itself will regress if there are too many breeders adopting such a haphazard approach to breeding. This summary of the way to plan your breeding program, assumes that you are breeding with the whole hearted goal of breeding the best dogs you possibly can, and not merely turning out puppies to supply the market demand.

1.  Study the MDBA approved Breed Description and in your mind's eye think of how you would like to see the dogs you breed look and act within five years or sooner. Think of a dog you greatly admire. Would you like the dogs you breed to be similar? If you would, stick a photo on your refrigerator or some other place where you will see it often, as a reminder of the goals you have set for yourself.

2.  If you already have Australian Cobberdog or Australian Labradoodle breeding stock, your first step should be to thoroughly assess your dogs as well as young puppies you have retained for future breeding. With an objective and unbiased eye, match the specific traits of each one of them with the  ideals outlined in the MDBA Breed Description. Make notes on the positive traits you want to keep in your progeny and on those which you would like to improve on. Be brutal.

3.  If you are just starting out as a breeder, then the first tip is also for you while you are deciding on which breeding stock will begin your breeding program.

4.  Remember that it isn't easy or even possible, to improve on too many specific characteristics all at the same time. Sometimes you will need to decide which undesirable trait irks you the most, and focus on that one first. If it compromises health, soundness or temperament, then it is top priority.

5.  Regardless of its bloodlines or pedigree, not every litter holds a puppy which is worthy of retaining for breeding. As you raise prospective breeding dogs, check on them for adherence to the MDBA Breed

Description. If they are not equal or better than their parents, try breeding the female to a different sire before you keep her progeny. If your stud dog produces inferior puppies to particular bloodlines, be responsible and only allow him to mate with other lines which have a better chance of success, or else neuter him.

6.  Dog breeding is an ever evolving process. To claim excellence because your dogs' pedigrees contain particular bloodlines or prestigious kennel names, is ignoring the fact that each individual dog is a living breathing creature with its own set of positive and negative qualities; some of them phonetic (what you see) and others genetically translated, even if you can't see them. Before you choose a stud dog for your female, evaluate the characteristics of each, and seek out how the dog you are considering has performed when bred to various bloodlines and types. In this way you will acquire the closest thing to a blueprint of what you may reasonably expect to produce in your own puppies.

# Breed Standard

## ABOUT BREED STANDARDS (BREED DESCRIPTIONS)

A breed standard or breed description is an articulate document which describes in detail how the ideal specimen in a specific dog breed, should look and behave. It is designed to provide a consistent, logical and enduring standard of excellence, intended to preserve the qualities of the breed, which make it suitable for the original purpose for which it was created. Adherence to the breed standard by breeders and show judges forms the guardianship of the breed's future.

In the case of a developing pure breed, what is known as a 'preliminary breed standard' is presented to the national kennel club monitoring the breed in the country of origin, taking into account that the emerging pure breed may still be passing through developmental changes which may require additions or amendments over time. The parent club is the only entity which is entitled to submit a preliminary breed standard and any future submissions for proposed changes or amendments. In the case of the Australian Cobberdog, its country of origin is Australia, and the kennel club body with the authority to accept or decline its preliminary breed standard as well as any proposed amendments or additions, is the Master

Dog Breeders and Associates,(MDBA) which is an international pure breed dog registry with its headquarters in Australia

Whilst a number of individuals and Labradoodle-specific registering bodies have designed their own varying breed standards over the past few years, unity is of the utmost importance and therefore a third party registering body is essential for the safeguarding of the breed's final acceptance as a recognised pure breed. The MDBA has sole autonomy to preside over the future of the Australian Cobberdog by way of its breed description as well as breeding protocols and ethics for its member breeders.

The Australian Cobberdog preliminary breed description places heavy emphasis on discouraging exaggeration of any feature of the dog. If for example, a feature is described as being 'broad' then 'broader' is deleterious and is penalised.

## PRELIMINARY BREED STANDARD
## 2013-AUSTRALIAN COBBERDOG

© The Australian and International Australian Cobberdog Club (AIACC)

### 1.  General Appearance:

A gracefully athletic and balanced dog, free of exaggeration, with a luxurious non-shedding coat which gives it ready access for its purpose as an assistance dog and therapy dog into places that may refuse entry to dogs with shedding coats. It's gentle nature, unique intuition which enables it to sense the emotional and physical needs of human beings and to act accordingly, together with its innate desire and aptitude for training, are expressed through its sociable and friendly nature, its desire for close human companionship and in its eyes which seek intimate contact with human eyes, and which should never be hidden by an overhang of its coat.

**2. Size, Proportion and Substance**:

Slightly off square, being a little taller than long when measured from the point of the shoulder to the rearmost projection of the upper thigh (point of buttocks). Boning is neither heavy nor fine but is sufficient to allow the dog to carry out the duties required of an assistance dog, with the least wear and tear on its body.

Miniature: 15ins – 18ins (38.1cm – 45.7cm)
Medium: 19ins – 22ins (48.3cm – 55.9cm)
Standard: 23ins – 26ins (58.4cm – 66cm)

**3. Head:**

Slightly square, free from exaggerations and in proportion to the size of the dog. Length from tip of nose to the inner corner of the eyes only slightly shorter than from the inner corner of the eyes to the point of the occiput. Nasal bones are broad and flat, with frontal bones a similar width to the side bones which have flat muscling giving a sculptured appearance. Skull gently rounded and of similar width to the frontal bones of the face.

Stop: blunt but well defined with a very slightly indented brow between the eyes.

Eyes: A Distinct Feature. Expression of the eyes is open, gentle, confident, and friendly. Round or oval, with long sweeping eyelashes and set well apart but not to the extreme side of the head. Expression and seeking intimate contact with human eyes is more important than exact shape. Eye colour and rich pigmentation of the rims blend with the surrounding coat.

Muzzle more broad than narrow, but not to excess. Lips firmly fitting and rims lined with unbroken pigment.

Bite: scissor or level bite

Teeth: strong and white with no discolouration or signs of wear.

Nose: A DistinctFeature. Noticeably large and fleshy with open nostrils and rich pigment.

Ears: Pendulous with long silky furnishings and a slightly elevated set-on at the base, which is only slightly above the outside corner of the eyes. Leather fine and pliable, with its tip at least mid way down the face, but not extending below the nose. Furnishings may extend below this point. Ear canals free from thick hair.

### 4,  Neck, Topline and Body

Neck: Elegant, with firm skin and a gentle arch. Flows naturally into the withers on the top, and down into the point of sternum on the under side without the appearance of being 'stuck on'.

Topline: Level with a slight rise over the loins to allow maximum reach and drive from the hindquarters.

Body: Free from exaggerations. Nothing should attract attention. Chest neither broad nor narrow, with brisket level with or slightly above the point of elbow. Ribs sufficiently well sprung to allow adequate heart and lung room. The back is level and strong from withers to the start of the flanks, with a slight rise of muscle over the loins to permit a long reaching drive from the hindquarters when gaiting. Tuck up is sufficient to enable the hind legs to reach well forward beneath the body when gaiting. The Croup only slightly tapers to the set on of tail.

Tail: Medium set on, plumed, sabre shaped without kinks and carried happily. The last two thirds may be above the dog's back when excited or in movement.

## 5. Forequarters

Shoulder blades are flat and layered with muscle. Angulation of the shoulders is symmetrical to that of the femur and tibia bones in the hindquarters, with sufficient slope to allow maximum extension of the front limbs when trotting. The point of shoulder is in line with the pro sternum. Upper arms are well muscled, with elbows neither pinched into the sides not protruding. Front legs are parallel to one another and straight to the ground with no deviation whether viewed from the front or the side. Cannons are strong and straight and only slightly longer than the relatively short and springy pasterns.

Feet: compact, either round or oval, with thick pads, well arched toes and short strong nails. Dewclaws are permitted on the front feet.

## 6. Hindquarters

Angulation of the femur and tibia bones is symmetrical to that of the scapula and humerus bones in the shoulders with sufficient slope to allow a long reaching propelling stride from the hind feet, which commences well forward beneath the body of the dog.

Thighs: upper thighs are broad, tapering only slightly into the second thigh. When viewed from the rear, the thighs are in a direct line behind the forearms of the front legs and are free of bowing or curvature.

Stifles: length is similar to that between point of elbow and pastern joint on the forequarters with sufficient angulation to smoothly transmit impulsion from the rear of the dog through to the front limbs.

Hock joint: strong, sinewy and broader than long

Hocks: strong and shorter rather than long. Close to the same length as the pasterns on the forequarters. Hocks are parallel to one another and straight to the ground when viewed from the rear or the side.

Feet: slightly more oval than the front feet. Compact, with thick pads, well arched toes and short strong nails. No dewclaws on the hind feet.

7. **Coat: A Distinct Feature. Single (no undercoat) non- shedding coat in either wool or fleece, with fleece preferred.**

Fleece: soft and luxurious to the touch, and ripples when the dog moves. Is not hair textured, not fuzzy curly or frizzy. Flows freely in soft waves of similar length and density up to approximately four inches (10.2 cm) long on the body, legs, head and face, and with a profusely plumed tail. The face is trimmed between and slightly above the eyes, the beard and coat on the cheeks are rounded off, with the areas beneath the ears, under the jaw and around the throat clipped short to permit adequate air flow. Paws are clipped out to the ankles, with the overhang hiding the clipped area and trimmed level with the ground. Clipping around the anal area beneath the tail is permitted in the interests of hygiene.

Wool: soft and luxurious to the touch and covers the entire body legs and head to about two inches (5.1 cm) in length, with fluffy curls which need trimming or clipping several times a year to be kept neat. The plumed tail is less curly than the rest of the dog. The face is trimmed between and slightly above the eyes, the beard and coat on the cheeks are rounded off, with the areas beneath the ears, under the jaw and around the throat clipped short to permit adequate air flow. Paws are clipped out to the ankles, with the overhang hiding the clipped area and trimmed level with the ground. Clipping around the anal area beneath the tail is permitted in the interests of hygiene.

Both coat types are expected to show discolouration and bleaching over the top coat, referred to as 'sunning' or 'weathering' as this breed is an active dog who enjoys the outdoors, and whose service work often requires him to spend a lot of time outside in all weathers. Discolouration of the top coat, or broken coat on the extremities are not penalised in the conformation show ring or other forms of competition. True colour can be determined by parting the coat with the hands and examining the colour the first two inches (5.1 cm) closest to the skin.

## 8. Colour

All colours are acceptable with the exception of Merles. Parti Colours have the same coloured eye and lip rims, and eye colour as their predominating colour.

Black dogs have black eye and lip rims, black noses and dark brown to black eyes

Silver dogs have black eye and lip rims, black noses and dark brown to black eyes

Cream dogs have black eye and lip rims, black noses and shades of brown eyes

Apricot dogs have black eye and lip rims, black noses and dark brown eyes

Red dogs have either black or red eye and lip rims and noses, and dark brown eyes

Chocolate, Café and Parchment dogs have liver eye and lip rims and noses, and hazel to amber eyes

Caramel dogs have liver eye and lip rims, noses, and hazel to amber eyes

Blue dogs appear black but have blue skin, and blue eye and lip rims. Eyes brown

Lavender is extremely rare and has pinkish to mauve skin, eye and lip rims and nose. Eyes hazel.

## 9. Gait: A Distinct Feature

Movement is the showcase of this breed's suitability as an active assistance or service dog where it is required to work for long periods without fatigue, and its movement is characterised by a joyous bearing, with a light footed, airy and tireless, long reaching and effortless stride that appears to float above the ground and to be going somewhere with purpose. The full trot is a true two-time action with no sign of ambling or pacing and the hocks do not wobble or bump together when viewed from the rear but move directly forward in line with the front legs. Seen from the side, the topline remains level with a minimum of up and down movement and the head and neck are extended rather than being unduly raised. Prancing mincing or high stepping are strongly penalised and each of the four legs steps forward long and low without dishing or plaiting.

## 10. Temperament and Nature: Distinct Features of Equal Importance

Temperament: happy, confident and sociable, extremely clever, calm, observant, easily trained, and adapts well to new situations and environments when handled with positive training techniques, but is easily discouraged by harsh training methods. Early training is quickly and keenly absorbed and is essential to avoid owners being outsmarted.

Nature: fun loving and clown-like with a keen sense of humour, sensitive and responsive to human emotion and physical incapacity, appears to be stubborn, when confused. Is happiest when living in close proximity to human family members and when it believes that it is serving them.

## 11. Faults:

Any departure from the foregoing points should be considered a fault and the seriousness with which the fault should be regarded should be in exact proportion to its degree and its effect upon the health and welfare of the dog and upon its ability to carry out the functions for which it was created.

# True Stories of Amazing Australian Cobberdogs

# Rusty and Captain Rick Doyle

My name is Captain Rick Doyle, and this is my true story about my Certified AssistanceDog Rusty. Rusty is an Australian Cobberdog bred by Beverley Manners of Rutland Manor in Australia and he came to me here in Hawaii in September2009 to help me to recover from cancer surgery and radiation. Without Rusty's love and support life would have been miserable these past few years. He gives me a reason to live!

He looks right into my eyes when I speak to him and he's developed a large vocabulary. He picks up anything he's shown almost immediately, and his intuition is amazing. In the early stages of my healing, he sensed right away that I needed help getting up the stairs and he'd pull me up to the top. Not long after we finished his training I started to swim again and Rusty knew when I was tired, and pulled me back to the beach while I hung onto his leash. When we swim now, he stays right by my side and has become a tremendous swimmer.

He's classically funny and has a hilarious sense of humour. When I ask him "Hey Rusty who's the most handsome dog in the world" Bark, Bark. "Hey Rusty, who's the smartest dog in the world." Bark Bark. Then he gives me a big high 5. "Hey Rusty, what's 2 + 1 equal? "Bark, Bark, Bark. He learned that in a matter of minutes. We leave crowds of people laughing on the beach each day. He brightens up every soul he meets. He treats everyone like his best friend. He's always been very gentle around small kids and babies without me ever having to tell him anything.

Rusty has comforted bereaved couples and I get letters from people that have met us thanking us for brightening up their days and for letting them meet Rusty. He's made so many friends here in Ko Olina. Everybody knows who he is. I've taken him everywhere I go and he's my best friend, companion and business partner. When we go to Costco everybody knows him by name. We go for walks here each day and since we live in a resort community he meets new people every day. He wants to greet everybody in the group and say hello to each one of them. When we depart he says goodbye to them all. He gives people hugs and kisses, that we call Rusty hugs. He's met 100's of dogs the past 3.5 years and he's nice to all of them, even the mean little ones that try to attack him. Rusty is the light and love of my life.

Captain Rick Doyle, 2013

# LEVI GIVES JOAN BACK HER LIFE

*How did I even live before Levi? If truth be told, life before Levi was not much of a life. In the weeks before we met face-to-face, I believed I could no longer cope with the all-over body pain and un- ending exhaustion that comes with having fibromyalgia. I not only wanted to give up by hiding under my blankets in bed, but I truly wanted my life to be over. I believed my chronic illness had been rendered me 'purpose-less' and I was, literally, researching the best way to end my life, when in 2007 I was notified by Canine Crossroads Foundation that Levi was ready for me and I should get myself to Texas for two solid weeks of service dog training with him ASAP. It's my firm belief that an angel named Beverley Manners, helped to facilitate the timing of that an- nouncement. What a blessing it has been!*

*Levi has enabled me to go out into the world, no longer fearing that folks will whisper, "Look at her loopy walk, she's drunk! What a shame!" or that I might fall and have no one to help me to get up. On the days that I am well, I'm half way decent. But before Levi came into my life, a flare up of symptoms would land me in a kind of hell. Levi has certainly changed all that. Now if I'm too ill   to do errands with him walking beside me, Levi seems content to lie next to me on my bed or sofa. He's ever ready to accompany me to the bathroom, offering the balance and support I need during those times, and even brings me my slippers, one by one. We move in smooth synchronicity. Often before I even utter a command or make a hand signal directing him, Levi senses my need or intention. As  my primary source of support for physical balance and item- retrieval, this 70-pound,  wavy-haired,  chocolate-colored Cobberdog helps me move through life with a grace and confidence  I thought I'd lost forever. Levi is so fully a part of my every motion, it's hard to believe we haven't always been together.*

*This handsome, kind, insightful and skilled dog has enabled me to re-enter the world and function in a way I thought had been taken from me forever. He has been the source of  my  personal renaissance and for that, I owe him my loyalty, love and care even beyond the time when we may no longer be able to walk together, side by side.*

*Joan Zatorski, Arizona*

# OSCAR SENSES EARTHQUAKE
# 5,000 KMS AWAY

*Oscar, our six month Australian Cobberdog that we purchased from Rutland Manor as a puppy, started frantically and uncharacteristically barking and growling at 7.50 am on Tuesday 22nd February 2011. He was running all over the house, and I called to him to stop barking but he persisted and ran outside, then back in again and appeared desperate to tell me something. Then he ran under my bed and lay there growling. It really was quite bizarre behaviour from a dog that hardly ever barks. Then I thought, it must be the smell of the jelly I was making so I tried to console him and showed him the empty box of jelly (he usually loves playing with empty boxes), but nope, he wasn't interested.*

*When I walked out of the bedroom he followed me and stood near the hallway to the back-door. Clearly, this time he was definitely trying to tell me something so I followed him and he ran outside and started barking and looking up on the roof of the house, so I praised him, thinking OK, there must be someone up on my roof, but nope, couldn't see anyone. I went around to the front of my house, but couldn't see anything strange. Then after a while he settled down and all was well.*

*About 30 minutes later I turned on the TV only to find out that at 12.51 pm (NZ time) Christchurch, in New Zealand had suffered through a huge earthquake. I phoned friends who I knew would know people over there and through a process of elimination determined that at the precise time that Oscar went crazy, was the time that New Zealand was experiencing the earthquake.*

*Now the confusing thing is, I have heard of dogs sensing when an earthquake is about to happen and they react but I live in Perth which is over 5,000 kms away and Oscar clearly demonstrated for 5-10 minutes quite disturbing behaviour. He knew something was wrong and was trying to tell me to get under the bed. So anyone who has one of these amazing dogs, listen to them. It just might save your life. What an incredible dog!*

*Barb and Keith Sutton and of course Oscar the Super-Dog Perth, Western Australia*

# ODI AND MARIE

*My Service Dog Odi is eight and a half years old. Odi was placed with me by Hawaii Fi-do Service dogs and his parents, Rex and Cocoa, were donated to Hawaii Fido by Beverley Manners of the Rutland Manor Breeding and Research Centre in Australia. He has been my Service Dog for seven years and we are still a strong team.*

*I am an RN who was unable to work due to multiple back surgeries and I have Neurological Lyme disease. I fall easily so I hold onto the handle on Odi's vest with my left hand to catch myself when I wobble and his leash in my right. When I do fall, the walker never lands close. Odi comes to me and I can get up by placing some of my weight carefully over his shoulders and if I need help Odi knows to run and find someone.*

*Last year I worked as the case manager for Developmentally Disabled adults in group homes. I often let Odi wander around as some of the residents loved his company. He was also an amazing resource. The staff knew there was an emergency, when he would run back and forth between me and a client and one time, he alerted them by barking loudly, just before someone had a seizure, giving them time to run to her side. There was one particular lady Odi normally ignored, but one day he went and sat by her, so it made me take a closer look. Her lungs were badly congested and I would not have known as I had not planned on assessing her that day. But Odi knew. When another lady fell, he voluntarily lay beside her on the floor until the ambulance came.*

*Odi visited hospitalised clients and lay on the bed next to them and he seemed to calm and comfort them more than medicine. The verbal clients ALL remembered his name, but rarely mine. I was "the nurse with MY dog." He accompanied them on outings and to their doctors' appointments, so if they wanted to claim ownership, it just made me smile*

*In the cardiac rehabilitation centre when patients were intimidated by the treadmill, Odi would get onto it, which made us all laugh and always got the patient to try the exercise. One very frail elderly man appeared in his usual state of health one session - all his vital signs and heart rhythms looked normal, yet Odi remained glued to his side, to the point of my reprimanding him as he was in the way. When the man suddenly became very ill, we were all shocked - but somehow yet again, Odi had picked up something we could not see. All of the patients loved him.*

*Odi always barked at one particular man and would have nothing to do with him. He visited several times because he had organised a children's colouring competition, with the winner getting a tour of his business. This man claimed to love dogs, but Odi acted so strangely around him that I made him lay under my desk whenever he was present. I apologized to the doctor one day and he said "Trust your dog. We have just learned that this man just got out of prison for child molestation." Occasionally, when I have been in a meeting, Odi would walk away from me and sit on someone's feet. They would always tell me afterwards that they were having a rough day and he sensed they needed him. Odi attends church, and the attendance record on the bulletin lists the number of people and 1 dog.*

*While Odi is my service dog, he also helps my family. Before I had him, they constantly checked up on my whereabouts if I was a moment late, which I found annoying. They now rely on Odi to help me get through each day. My husband cares about him as much as I do; he cuts his hair, trims his nails, and is the person Odi goes to when he wants to be scratched. Our entire town adores Odi. He has given me my life back. I would not be independent without his patient assistance each day.*

*Sincerely, Marie Wachsmuth and Odi, Oregon USA*

# MEGGIE AND CHARLOTTE — AN INTERNATIONAL FIRST

*Meggie and Charlotte*

*Photo Courtesy Erich Snijder*

*Meggie, (Rutlands Lil Keira) born October 2005 at Rutland Manor in Australia, was the first dog of her breed to compete in the Dutch National Agility Championships in June 2013.*

*In April 2013 at age seven and a half, Meggie won the Provincial Agility Championships in Holland. She competed in the Dutch National Team Championships in June 2013 and her clear rounds on both the Jumping and the Agility resulted in a number one ranking in Agility and a 7th place overall. Meggie is now the provincial champion 2013 and she competes nationally in the highest league. When she arrived in the Netherlands, it was mutual love at first sight. Right from the start it was clear that our girl would one day become a real athlete. Her athletic build, and incredible capacity to concentrate on the job at hand would one day turn this bundle of joy into the perfect agility dog for me. When she finished her last Obedience exam I took her to an agility class and was asked to let her compete in the provincial and later on in the national league. I felt afraid of failure, but Meggie gave me the self-confidence I needed to go on!*

*Meggie is not only agility to us. She is a wonderful family member. She loves to go camping with us. Her favourite activities are going to the beach to catch her frisbee, diving into the waves to fish her ball out of the sea and running along the French canals on the tow path while we paddle the boat.*

*We have two mentally challenged people in our family, one of whom is also physically challenged, and Meggie is extremely gentle with them. She is very comfortable with walking alongside a wheelchair and she does not impose herself. So she is also a perfect companion in a program for visiting senior citizens,and psychiatric patients. There is absolutely nothing that we do not like about her. We love her!*

*Charlotte Van der Vorst Holland*

*Meggie's trophy array*

# AMBER BELLA AND JOYCE BRING CHEER TO YOUNG AND OLD

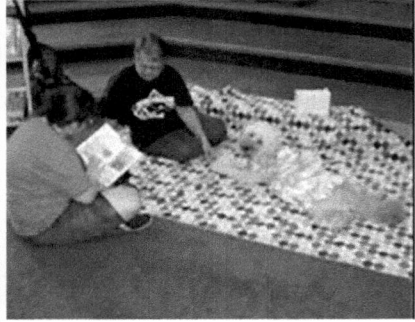

*Amber CGC at 6months and Certified Therapy Dog at 9months Bella: Certified Therapy Dog at 5months.*

*Rutlands Lil Amber is an Australian Cobberdog born at Rutland Manor Breeding and Research Center in Australia. She arrived here in California on December 20, 2003 and was the best Christmas present anyone ever received. From the first day I picked her up she was the most outgoing, self-assured dog I have ever owned. Even after her long flight from Melbourne she was not afraid or timid in any way. She simply wanted out of her crate to say hello to everyone she encountered.*

*In April I signed Amber and I up for an orientation and testing session with the local therapy dog organization – PAWS for Healing in Napa, California. Amber was only six months old and I had no expectation that she would pass the testing. To my considerable amazement, Amber passed all of the tests with flying colors! At this time we were approached by the local public library's librarian. She was interested in starting a R.E.A.D program. I found the idea intriguing so I began working with the librarian to put together a program. The whole idea is that the child reads aloud to the dog who is not judgmental, and who won't correct or laugh or make the child feel uncomfortable. All of the*

*R.E.A.D. dogs must first be Certified Therapy Dogs. In addition they must be calm and relaxed enough to sit quietly while the child is reading. They are taught several commands which will lead the child to believe that the dog is focused on the book and actually paying attention to the reader.*

*First we both had to be trained for R.E.A.D. and in turn, train other volunteer therapy teams. After six months of opposition, politicking and endless meetings we finally gained permission and held a press conference to announce the initial program. Amber and Bella are both certified R.E.A.D dogs but Amber was the first one in this area nearly 9 years ago. I can tell you that not only was the program successful – it was wildly so. The kids LOVED it! The parents LOVED it, especially when they started seeing the results of the program-increased confidence in reading aloud being the most obvious one. In no time we were receiving requests from other libraries who wanted to do the program. We now have Paws For Reading programs in every library in Solano County, California of which there are 11. We are also in every Napa County public library and in Sonoma County as well. In addition to the public libraries we are in many elementary schools and boys and girls clubs throughout the area. Now our Paws For Reading program is in every public library in the 3 counties we serve and in many elementary schools.*

*When Bella came to me she too, surpassed all my expectations, gaining her certification as a Therapy Dog at the age of five months. She also became a R.E.A.D dog and both dogs enjoy their library visits. The children are tickled to learn that Amber and Bella are first cousins and both came from Australia. It's hard to believe that Amber is nearly 10 at this point. While she is not showing signs of slowing down at all, the R.E.A.D program is wonderful for senior therapy dogs. It is not physically taxing and they get to enjoy being with the kids! A wonderful way to extend a therapy career.*

*I also work with seniors, Alzheimer patients and a local hospital which is in my neighborhood. So many of our seniors get no visitors whatsoever and are doomed to a life of loneliness and depression. Many of them have told me that they so look forward to our visits that it gives them a reason to get up in the morning. Helping these people even one day a week is something that is rewarding beyond my ability to express. Little Amber and Bella bring joy to all of these people and enrich my life every day of the week. I thank God for bringing them to me.*

*Joyce Bristow*
*Vacaville, California*

# Judy Suan and UB

*This is a true story of one of those especially bred dogs of the authentic breed of Australian Labradoodle, a dog named UB. He was born on the island of Kauai at Paradise Labradoodles and his parents came from the Rutland Manor Labradoodle breeding and Research Centre in Australia, the co-founder of the breed. UB was donated to Hawaii Fido Service Dogs to be raised and trained as an assistance dog.*

*He was flown to Oahu at a young age and started training in obedience in schools and hospitals and when he was 1 ½ years of age he was placed in my care as a pup in training under my Labrador Jazzy to see if he had potential as a Medical Alert Service Dog. He would follow Jazzy's lead and before long was responding to my every need alerting me if my blood pressure or heart rate rose. UB's life was beginning as a service dog as we completed the six months' probationary advanced skills training before becoming a Certified Medical Alert/Brace Service Dog, with public access to accompany me any where I go on aeroplanes, into grocery stores, to doctor visits, football games, theatres and work.*

*I had learned from my grandmother that animals and nature would help to keep me centred and calm. I hadn't realised that my special energy had a name given to it; ADHD with hyperactivity, until I was an adult teaching Special Education. With the assistance of my service dog I have eliminated the need for medication and my panic anxiety attacks have reduced in frequency. UB has taught me to relax and take slow cleansing breathes to calm my mind and muscles.I feel blessed by my angel and service dog named UB. Mahalo, Thank you for reading our story.*

*Submitted by Judy Suan and UB*
*Certified Medical Alert/Brace Service Dog TEAM*
*Accredited with Assistance Dogs International*
*With Hawaii Fido Service Dogs*
*Volunteer Coordinator/Kennel Manager/Public Awareness Director since 2000*

# LOUDDLE RECOGNISED BY ROYALTY

R.I.P. LOUDDLE 1994 – 2010

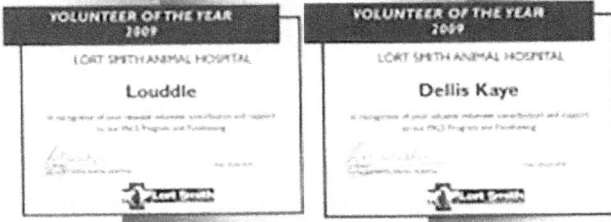

*Our Australian Labradoodle 'Louddle' came home to us from Rutland Manor early February 1995 and that was the start of the most wonderful union with Louddle. She was a delight from the very first moment and travelled home with us so happy and relaxed. We arrived home to two more dogs and all the cats, but that was no problem, they all got along very happily together.*

*Louddle was the most wonderful dog anyone could have, and she was probably the first certified Therapy dog of her breed in Australia and began visiting Hazelbean Nursing Home Williamstown in 1998. Three major Melbourne hospitals gave Louddle her own official I.D. Louddle had a very special story with Annie at Marina. They had a very close bond and when Annie passed away Louddle was asked   to her funeral and followed Annie being carried out of the church. Louddle could not go into the room Annie had occupied for some months later. When Louddle passed away, a rose from Annie was placed with her.*

*It's not every day that a dog earns its human parents the honour of meeting royalty, but that's exactly what Louddle did for us in November 2012. Prince Charles and the Duchess of Cornwall flew to Australia to attend the Melbourne Cup, 'The Horse Race that Stops the Nation' at Flemington Racecourse in Melbourne, and we were invited to meet them personally to honour Louddle for her fifteen years of outstanding service in charity fundraising and hospital visitations.*

*Louddle was in high demand for TV shows, Fashion Parading, Football Mascotting, Festivals and competitions, and raised many thousands of dollars for her charities. Louddle retired  from  her  busy working life at age fifteen, and her retirement was marked by many people contacting us to tell us stories about what a difference she had made to their family member.*

*Graeme and I were both asked to the Lort Smith Annual Meeting, which was unusual. After the formalities were over, pictures of Louddle came up on a large screen (we had wet eyes) and then the biggest shock when Louddle was posthumously  awarded "Volunteer of the Year 2009". I received the same award also, but Graeme and I were so proud of Louddle we cried with happiness.  We had lost Louddle only one month before at age sixteen. It was such a very proud time to think she was thought so highly of for her years of work for Lort Smith Animal Hospital.*

*14 yr old Louddle with Graeme and Dellis, re-visit*
*Beverley Manners at Rutland Manor July 2007*

## MY FRIEND ANNIE ELIZABETH BERRYMAN
### By LOUDDLE
**Courtesy of Her Human Parents Graeme and Dellis Kaye**

*Annie with Louddle on Annie's 102nd Birthday*

*This is my most treasured story about a very special lady, Annie (Annie Elizabeth Berriman 1906-2008). I have met a lot of people with my visits to Hazeldeen Williamstown Hospital-Marina, but Annie and I had an unspoken love. I started visiting Marina at North Altona every Monday afternoon, about the same time Annie went to live there. I would shake hands with Annie and she would give me Schmackos and on each visit she would be sitting in her chair by the window. We celebrated Annie's one hundred and first birthday on 13th March 2007 and Annie was still well enough to move around her room unaided and to walk to the dining room with the help of a walking frame.*

*On Annie's one hundred and second birthday, she woke to balloons in her room and I visited her with flowers. Annie was dressed up in a frock with white dots because she said they matched the balloons she had woken to. It was a very happy march day in 2008. One Thursday on 8th May 2008, we were not rostered to visit, but we did so as a fill-in, and as I entered Annie's room she was not in her chair, but in bed. I walked with all my strength to the far side of her bed, and sat beside it and my mother Dellis plaed Annie's hand on my head. Annie knew me but she was very weak and as her hand slipped off my head, I placed my paw on her hand, with all my strength and love. I gave Annie my love until I was panting so hard, and with a kiss on her hand I left. We had said our goodbyes.*

*The next day I could not eat and on Saturday morning we got a 'phone call to tell us that Annie had passed away on the Friday 9th May 2008. I was invited to Annie's funeral which was held at St Stephens Uniting Church Williamstown and as I was getting out of the car, friends of Annie came up to meet me. To my surprise, a photo of Annie and me was on the order of service. Annie was a lady with so much love, and so much love around her, a truly beautiful person.*

*Louddle*

# About the Author

B everley Rutland-Manners was born in Sydney Australia into an urban environment that did little to ignite the passion for animals that was to mark her life's work. After completing her scholarly studies she moved away from the cities and into rural regions where she was more able to combine practical and hands-on animal husbandry with her research into animal welfare and health. Typically a pioneer by nature, Beverley was responsible for initiating many of the present day protocols including health screening for breeding dogs, which are now considered usual practice in Australia and abroad. Internationally acclaimed as an animal behaviourist and premier dog trainer and breeder, she has never been content to rest on her laurels, and continues to focus on keeping up to date with modern day veterinary advances and on mentoring others. Beverley continues to breed her beloved Australian Cobberdogs and her puppies are prized in seventeen countries across the world.

# Endnotes

1. John Bryant, Fettered Kingdoms: An Examination of A Changing Ethic,1982:15

2. Ingrid Newkirk, PETA's founder and president, New Yorker Magazine, April 23, 2003

3. Tom Regan, 'Animal Rights, Human Wrongs' speech given at University of Wisconsin, Madison, October 27, 1989.

4. http://www.trentonian.com/article/TT/20061223/TMP02/312239988

5. Screaming Wolf (pseudonym), A Declaration of War: Killing People to Save Animals and the Environment. Patrick Henry Press, 1991

6. http://www.naiaonline.org/

7. Dr Jean Dodds D.V.M. (1994) "Guide to Congenital and Heritable Disorders in Dogs", published by The Humane Society Veterinary Medical Association August 1994

8. Dr Jean Dodds D.V.M. (1997) "Guide to Congenital and Heritable Disorders in Dogs", published by The Humane Society Veterinary Medical Association, revised August 1997.

9. As mentioned before it is important to distinguish between crossbreeding and infusing into established bloodlines. Infusions are not crossbreeding.

10. Dr W. Jean Dodds D.V.M. (2004) Guide to Congenital and Heritable Disorders in Dogs. Published by The Humane Society Veterinary Medical Association.

11. Veterinary Genetic Assurance program (VGA) Website. http://vetga.com.au/page14/page14.html

12. Dr W.Jean Dodds D.V.M. (2011) Guide to Congential and Heritable Disorders in Dogs Includes Genetic Predisposition to Diseases Published by The Humane Society Veterinary Medical Association Revised May 2011.
[*] Yvonne and Ricky are pseudonyms used to protect the individuals' identities.

13. I incorporated the LAA in Victoria on June 14, 2000. Incorporation No: AC039798P

14. Bijal P Trivedi, National Geographic Reporting Your World Daily, 'What's a Labradoodle - Designer Dog or Just Another Mutt?' Published February 9, 2004.

15. Business Wire, Duluth, Minn. Maurices Introduces Limited Edition Lucky the Labradoodle Plush Dog to Support American Cancer Society. November 29,2005

16. Reuters New York 'Lord & Taylor Presents $55,000 Check to Guiding Eyes from Holiday Fund Raiser'. Sept 14, 2006.

17. Reuters, New York 'The Old Shoe is Gone' by Gertrude Chavez-Dreyfuss, September 14, 2006.

18. Dodds, W. Jean & Stefanon, Bruno (2009) 'Nutrigenomics as it relates to skin', Proceedings of the American Holistic Veterinary Medical Association, Annual Conference in Fitchburg, MA pp.66-70.

19. www.nutriscan.org

www.ingramcontent.com/pod-product-compliance
Lightning Source LLC
Chambersburg PA
CBHW051245020426
42333CB00025B/3067